THE ART STUDENT SURVIVAL GUIDE

JEFFREY K. OTTO
The Art Institute of Philadelphia

THOMSON

DELMAR LEARNING Australia Canada Mexico Singapore Spain United Kingdom United States

THOMSON
DELMAR LEARNING

The Art Student Survival Guide
Jeffrey Otto

Vice President, Technology and Trades SBU:
Alar Elken

Editorial Director:
Sandy Clark

Senior Acquisitions Editor:
James Gish

Development Editor:
Jaimie Wetzel

Marketing Director:
Dave Garza

Channel Manager:
William Lawrensen

Marketing Coordinator:
Mark Pierro

Production Director:
Mary Ellen Black

Production Manager:
Larry Main

Production Editor:
Thomas Stover

Cover Design:
Chris Navetta

Cover Production:
David Asenault

Illustrator:
Jeffrey K. Otto

Library of Congress Cataloging-in-Publication Data:

ISBN: 1-4018-4365-4

NOTICE TO THE READER

Contents

iii

Preface

Intended Audience

This book is designed for students who will be or are majoring in art at the college or university level. Whether it is at a small private art school, a community college, or a major university, the success or failure of the student often has less to do with talent and more to do with how he or she handles the experience of being an art student. This book is targeting all art students, especially those enrolled in freshman seminar courses. High school art teachers and guidance counselors may find it helpful when working with juniors and seniors preparing to be art majors in college. It may also be useful to students who are having problems with their grades or staying in school.

Art school can be the high point of one's life or a waste of time and money. By utilizing the information and techniques in this book, students can make the most of their time in art school and be able to look back on it from a successful career with fond memories of a great adventure they once had.

BACKGROUND OF THIS TEXT

I have been associated with artists in higher education my entire adult life. Ten years spent as an art student has earned me Bachelor of Arts, Master of Arts, and Master of Fine Arts degrees. I have worked with many instructors and professors during that time. Some were good, some not so good. I have spent another 12 years in the classroom/studio as a professor of illustration and computer graphics, and 6 more years as an administrator in an art college. I have worked with thousands of art students over the years and stayed in touch with more than a few of them. I have heard the stories of what they have gone through just to survive being an art student, and I have witnessed firsthand the success or lack of success many of them have experienced.

One observation I have made over time is that successful art students set up work habits and behaviors that make it easier for them to become successful artists. So that is where I must begin, with new art students. This book is for them—a book that contains tools and tips that will make that journey through art school a little smoother. It is a journey about survival and success, a journey that will lead to a successful career as an artist.

Because not all high schools and school districts fund the arts equally, students enter college with quite a broad range of experiences. Foundation classes help get everyone on the same page as far as the basics of art and design are concerned. This book provides some additional help to art students, help that is not always taught or available in the classroom. It is intended to help make the journey through art school a little less frantic and a little more inspired. It is a reference guide designed to address the balance of time, energy, money, and creativity required to get through art school. The only requirements needed to use this book are the ability to read and the desire to succeed.

ORGANIZATION

The Art Student Survival Guide is divided into three major sections. Part 1: The Basics, contains information that is a combination of common sense and study skills. It lays the groundwork for becoming a successful student. Part 2: The Techniques, covers a few drawing basics and some design tips. There is also a chapter that deals with creative problem solving and includes good solid approaches for working up strong solutions. Part 3: The Tools, refers to the tools and supplies used in the studio and ways of setting up a work space. The book is rounded out with a catch-all chapter on miscellaneous stuff. Each chapter is filled with numerous illustrations.

Part 1: The Basics

✔ Chapter 1, "Tick, Tick, Tick, Tick...," is the chapter dedicated to time and time management. Included here are techniques to budget time so all the homework is done, done well, and all deadlines are met with minimal stress. Managing time is many an art students' nightmare. Spending hours on a drawing, only to crumple it up and toss into the basket, then doing it again, and again, and again . . . the creative process doesn't always come easily, and the solution sought is not always ready to surface when needed. Learn to know and recognize how long things really take to be done right.

✔ Chapter 2, "Keeping It Together," addresses health issues both physical and mental including diet, sleep, and exercise. It discusses emotional issues, spiritual issues, and stress, looking at how all of these can affect students and their work. It also addresses the bigger picture—life and how life outside of school can affect life in school.

✔ Chapter 3, "How It's Done and How to Do It," contains useful tips and tools for studying. It covers what demos are and how they can differ from course to course. It discusses the critique, how to prepare for it, and how to react to it. Also included are note-taking tips for slide lectures and computer software demonstrations and using a sketchbook journal as a study tool and vehicle for documenting creative projects.

✔ Chapter 4, "Relationships with Peers, Faculty, and Advisors," discusses the importance of establishing good people skills and using them to one's advantage in school. Coverage includes taking advice and the responsibility for the advice taken; getting to know one's peers and experiencing life with others; positioning one's self for success by establishing good relationships with teachers, administrators, and advisors; and networking.

Part 2: The Techniques

✔ Chapter 5, "Some Design Basics," is just that, the basics. Since students will be taking basic design courses, this chapter is included as a reminder for some and a brief introduction for others. The elements of design—point, line, shape, texture, color, and basic composition techniques—are presented as well as the concepts of symmetry and stability.

✔ Chapter 6, "Drawing the Human Figure," contains a brief look at the basics of drawing the human figure. Many art students will take a course in figure drawing, and this chapter provides a basic overview of drawing with important information on working with models. Discussed in this chapter are the robot, the gesture, line of action, and movement. Also included are techniques of drawing hands, feet, and faces, as well as measuring while drawing.

✔ Chapter 7, "Creative Problem Solving," looks at a few of the lessons that I have used over the years to help students break through a creative block or generate interesting ideas for projects. Techniques include working with word games, lists of adjectives, possible but not probable occurrences, and using memory and imagination.

Part 3: The Tools

✔ Chapter 8, "Tools of the Trade," reminds the reader that even in these days of computers in the arts, there are many other artists' tools that still hold their own in the studio. A look at the basic tools used in foundation level courses will inform those who have not worked with them before and also remind those who have that there is a tool for each job and the importance of using it.

✔ Chapter 9, "Setting Up Your Studio," covers the importance of having a place to work and keep art supplies. Establishing a studio area, and topics such as light, electric, ventilation, expense, furniture, and location are discussed. Using basic techniques of feng shui, co-ops and sharing spaces, and expenses are also mentioned.

✔ Chapter 10, "The Digital Chapter," gives a brief look at issues that accompany digital work in the studio. This chapter is not about specific computers or software, but is about working with the tools available without fear of corruption or failure. Basic information regarding working with digital media, including saving, backing up, organizing, archiving, and storing files is provided. Topics also presented in this chapter are labeling, dating work, when to buy a computer and what to buy, and ergonomics and health hazards.

✔ Chapter 11, "Miscellaneous Stuff," is just that. Here you will find bits of information that don't really fit in the other chapters but are useful just the same. This section is a collection of useful tools, including basic ruler reading (you would be surprised how many college students can't read a ruler), fraction-to-decimal conversion charts (useful for layout and design work on computers), basic one-, two-, and three-point perspective diagrams, and sources of inspiration.

FEATURES

The following list provides some of the salient features of the text:

- ✔ Provides advice on avoiding the common pitfalls experienced by first year art students
- ✔ Discusses how to find the right balance amid all the new demands of being an art student
- ✔ Gives examples of different note-taking techniques for different studio or class situations
- ✔ Includes a useful review of the elements of design and common drawing techniques
- ✔ Contains a knowledgeable look at technology— showing students how the digital world will shape their work as artists and preparing them for making the most of the software programs they will need to learn

ABOUT THE AUTHOR

Jeffrey K. Otto is academic director of the Media Arts and Animation Department at the Art Institute of Philadelphia. In addition to 12 years of experience as a professor of computer graphics and illustration, Otto has been an art administrator for 6 years and has more than 20 years of experience as a designer/illustrator and fine artist working in both traditional and new media.

Working in digital media since 1986, he is quite familiar with teaching graphic software applications. In the computer lab, he has taught introductory and intermediate levels of computer graphics, digital layout, image processing, and digital illustration. In the classroom, his philosophy is to nurture and encourage thinking artists. In the traditional studio, he has taught drawing, painting, printmaking, and multiple levels of illustration.

In 1995 Otto was the curator of "The Book of Icons and Other Digital Addictions," a national computer art exhibition at the Walt Whitman Cultural Arts Center in Camden, New Jersey. Jurors of the exhibit included John Ittman, curator of prints from the Philadelphia Museum of Art and Rick DeCoyte, owner of Silicon Gallery, Philadelphia, Pennsylvania.

In 1997 he presented a multimedia lecture "Mixing Digital and Traditional Media" at the 17th annual symposium on small computers in the arts at the Franklin Institute Science Museum in Philadelphia. His fine art has been exhibited at the San Bernardino Museum, the Franklin Institute Science Museum, the Winterthur Museum, and regional Philadelphia galleries. His commercial clients have included Ryder Truck Rental, New York Power Authority, Philadelphia Inquirer Magazine, Consolidated Freightways, and Office Systems Magazine.

Jeff Otto is also a member of the College Art Association.

ACKNOWLEDGMENTS

It is very important that acknowledgments and thanks be given to those who were instrumental in the creation of this project, for without their help, support, and guidance, this book would not have been possible.

Thanks go to my instructors, professors, and students for their inspiration and the experiences I had with them that eventually become the source of the content for this book.

Thanks to Howard B. Kinch and William Derek Rhodarmer for the vintage fountain pens that I used to create the drawings in this book.

Thanks to Bradley Keough for sharing his illustrated "Colonel Rick's Stone Soup" poster.

Thanks to my daughter Natalie for the many hours that she spent researching museums and galleries.

Thanks to the staff at Thomson Delmar Learning especially:

Jim Gish, Senior Acquisitions Editor, for helping direct my vision into a topic that I could write an entire book on, to his faith in the project, and his musical inspiration.

Jaimie Wetzel, Developmental Editor, for her guidance, kind nature, and patience, which I'm sure I tried on more than one occasion.

Tom Stover, Production Editor, for directing the production of this book while keeping my own artistic vision in mind.

PREFACE

Thomson Delmar Learning and the author would also like to thank the following reviewers for their valuable suggestions and expertise:

Vickey Bolling
Graphic Design Department
Art Institute of Atlanta
Atlanta, Georgia

Kevin Hedgpeth, Assistant Academic Director
Media Arts and Animation, Game Art and Design,
    and Multimedia and Web Design
Art Institute of Phoenix
Phoenix, Arizona

Suzanne Manheimer, Chair
Graphic Design Department
Art Institute of California—Los Angeles
Santa Monica, California

Francisco Virella, Academic Director
Media Arts and Animation, Multimedia and Web Design
Art Institute of Las Vegas
Henderson, Nevada

Jeffrey K. Otto
2004

Questions and Feedback

Thomson Delmar Learning and the author welcome your questions and feedback. If you have suggestions that you think would benefit others, please let us know and we will try to include them in the next edition.

To send us your questions and/or feedback, you can contact the publisher at:

Thomson Delmar Learning
Executive Woods
5 Maxwell Drive
Clifton Park, NY 12065
Attn: Graphic Arts Team
800-998-7498

Or the author at:

Art Institute of Philadelphia
1622 Chestnut Street
Philadelphia, PA 19103
jotto@aii.edu

Introduction

Like a trip west without a map, you can simply follow the setting sun and eventually get there. Or you can use a map, plan a route, and leave less to chance. Make the most of the experience. Would you embark on a major trip without a road map? Think of art school as a journey and this book as a road map or travel guide. It will help you make the most of the experience, for you are about to start a great adventure, one that will be filled with awesome discoveries and frustrating obstacles. You will meet people along the way who will become lifelong friends and others who will grate on your every nerve.

Some people will drive cross-country without a map. They want the adventure and freedom to go with the flow. Some of them may eventually get there and have great experiences along the way. Others may not reach their final destination at all, missing out on some of the best that the country has to offer. Those who plan out their trip, the ones who prepare by talking to others who have made the journey already, the ones who have done their homework and have a clue as to what's ahead will find the gems along the way that others may cruise right past. They will make the most of the trip and in the process, prepare themselves for the next great adventure that comes after school, life as an artist.

My involvement with art in higher education began in the 1970s. My experiences include those of undergraduate student, graduate student, faculty member, advisor, area coordinator, and department chair. I have had the good fortune to attend and work in a variety of institutions, ranging from state college to arts university. All along the way I have been with art students. I have seen the good ones and I have seen the not-so-good ones. My experiences in school have been from both sides of the table. I have been the immature undergraduate student, I have been the serious graduate student, and I have been the concerned advisor. Fortunately I have learned from all of my experiences in school, and through this book I want to share some of those lessons.

There are talented students, some serious as nails. There are less talented ones who also have the drive and desire to succeed. Then there were the talented ones who end up in school for the party—students who have the ability but just do not have the maturity needed to be successful yet. Many factors play a part in whether a student works to his or her maximum potential. The major chosen does not guarantee success. Nor does attending a "better" school. There is no guarantee that anyone will be a success.

One question that is not asked enough is "Are you ready for college?" or "Am I ready to be a serious student?" Being a high school graduate has very little to do with being ready for college. It takes drive, ambition, maturity, and goals. The school you choose is not as important as the energy you put into your education.

INTRODUCTION

The energy put into education often deals with priorities and maturity. Remember why you are going to school; remember what it is going to cost. If you are not ready yet, take some time to get ready. You'll be glad you did.

As artists we use labels to identify what we work with, what we do, and why we do it. Sculptors, painters, potters, animators, designers, illustrators, printmakers, architects, photographers, and the rest—we are all labeled. Even colleges and universities have developed their own labels such as Visual Communications, Interactive Design, and New Media. Yet a common factor ties us all together— the need to express and explore the spirit of the creative process that originates in our hearts and our souls.

I have been fortunate to work as a fine artist, commercial artist, and arts educator, and in each case I have felt that creative energy. The more I do, the more artists I speak with, the more students that I work with, the more I see that while we are all very different, we are all very much the same, and that the title "artist" is a sufficient title for all of us. This book is for all of you artists about to make the journey.

This book is dedicated to all of the artists, arts educators, and art students who were the inspiration for it, and to my family and friends for their love and support.

PART

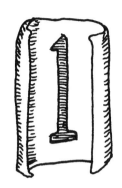

The Basics

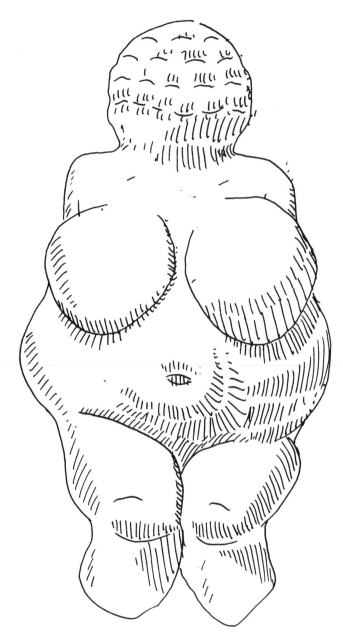

Venus of Willendorf, c. 25,000–20,000 BC

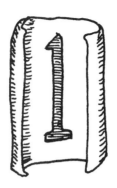

Tick, Tick, Tick, Tick . . .

✔ Finding Balance

✔ Time Management

✔ How Long Things Really Take

✔ Getting Organized

✔ Stay On Task

It's all about time. There are only so many hours in the day. No matter how much you wish there were more, there are only 26 hours in a day . . . umm 25 . . . no 24 . . . that's it, 24 hours in a day. How you survive and succeed in art school may come down to how well you use your time.

FINDING BALANCE

Because there are a limited amount of hours in a day, you will have to practice the time-honored tradition of "give and take." If you are fortunate enough to be in the position that you do not have to work while in school, take advantage of this opportunity; <u>do not</u> take it for granted. You have an edge, don't waste it. The older you get, you will see that time does indeed fly. Life is too short to waste time.

When entering art school or college majoring in art, you will find yourself stretched thin, if you are "doing it right." If this is your first time away from home, you will be learning how to live on your own, maybe in a dorm setting, maybe with a roommate—a roommate who snores or has stinky feet or has a girlfriend who is always visiting. Maybe this roommate is a slacker or maybe a total bookworm. What about food? Who cooks? Do you eat in a cafeteria or do you send for take out? Is your diet restricted? Are you a picky eater? Are you a morning person or a night owl? If you don't already know, this is a good time to try to get an idea of what type of person you are.

Some people are punctual, some are early birds, and some are late, always late. Not just students, but kids, parents, and even teachers can run late (or early) as the case may be. Ever notice students trying to sneak into the class after it started? They are trying not to draw attention to themselves, but it rarely works. All it takes is one person to turn and look. That can cause a domino effect that surely will give away the tardy culprit. And once this happens the instructor has lost the class's attention. Not a good way to make points with an instructor.

When you were a child, one of your parents may have been your alarm clock. At school, your days were planned; bells rang to signal your next task, class, or activity. Even extracurricular activities were planned and only ran a certain amount of time. Life was scheduled. As a college student be prepared to follow the schedule that the school is using, and remember your priorities. All of these variables—maturity issues, compatibility, different backgrounds, temperaments, and tastes—add to the

5

pressures of being an art student. And these things can make life away from home difficult.

TIME MANAGEMENT

Managing time is many an art student's nightmare. Many hours are spent on a drawing, only to crumble it up and toss into the basket, then doing it again, and again, and again. We've all done that. The creative process does not always come easily, and the solution sought is not always ready to surface when needed. To get so lost in work that hours fly by as minutes, then suddenly find out that the entire night has been spent on one project, while other assignments also due sit unfinished is the curse of the art student. College art students may be balancing three or four studio classes, learning new software, even taking math or physics courses all at the same time. And that's just school. Toss into the mix a part-time job, a social life, family, friends, and romance. Too much of any one of these can be deadly to the mix. Learn how to own time, how to make it work for you.

Time management is a concept foreign to many but beneficial to those who do it well. It eludes many students. After all, how often have you started work on a project only to look up at the clock and see that it is 3 a.m., not 11:30 as you expected? (If you have not experienced this yet, don't worry, you will.) And how many times have you started something only to erase it and start again, and erase it and start again, and erase it and start again . . . ?

It is hard enough to keep track of time and balance your work schedule without the redo haunting you. You must learn to keep track of time and I don't mean wearing a watch. Find a way to track time. One successful technique that I have found is the use of a kitchen timer. The timer on a computer can also work, but the downside to that is you will not always be using digital or electronic equipment. A good old battery-operated kitchen timer will do just fine. How about the ancient technology of the hourglass, reminding us how time can slip through our hands like the sands of time. They all work. Try one, try them all, try to budget your time. Plan

7

your day to include time not only for homework, but time to go to class (include commuting time if needed), time to eat, time to relax, time to work your job, time to sleep, maybe even a little time to waste. Don't forget to schedule time for social activities. But how do you schedule time for being sick, or tired? Then if you are sick and miss all of the other things you've scheduled time for, how do you schedule time to make up what you've missed?

✔ Make a list of things to do and set your priorities.

✔ Try to start with a time budget, estimating how much time can or should be used on a project.

✔ Keep a timecard for your projects, maybe on the back of the project or in your sketchbook.

✔ Use a 9 X 12 envelope for each project, put related papers in it and write notes and hours worked on it.

✔ Use scheduled broadcast programs on TV or radio as time markers.

✔ Listen to CDs while working and then add up total time of CDs played.

You can try to map it out and have a chart, or you can use your 75-function digital watch or cell phone. Some people use a personal digital assistant (PDA); some people use a day-timer. Each can provide a calendar, an address book, and even a calculator. But having one is only good if you use it. This means making it a part of your daily routine. Ultimately what you are doing is making and using a good old-fashioned list.

For years the list has been used by many. Some people start each day making a "things to do" list while they have their breakfast or morning caffeine fix. Some people like to plan out tomorrow and set their next day's goals before they go to bed at night. Try to make your school schedule (when you have a choice) one that you can realistically accomplish. Look at the calendar, make a list, start being aware of time. Estimating time is not an easy task, or at least an easy task to do well. It is important to have an idea of how long things really take to do.

HOW LONG THINGS REALLY TAKE

I can always count on e-mails or calls from students and grads alike with the same question—How much should I charge for this project? It's pretty easy to figure out. That last great project you did is the one that got you this project. How long did that one take? Multiply those hours by your hourly rate and there you have it, or at least a pretty good starting point. Keep track of how long it takes to do something. This can only be done as you work. Trying to backtrack days or weeks remembering hours is not an exact science. But if you keep a piece of paper with the project or write the hours on the back of the project or in your sketchbook, or in your Day-Timer, you will soon find out that what you thought was 8 hours is really 14 hours. See if there is a pattern. Are you doing something faster or slower than you realized? Are there any bottlenecks in the production process?

Record all the time spent on research, sketching, drawing, revising, painting, sculpting, shooting, etc. You should be keeping track of cost as well. Did you have to run to the store to get supplies? How much do those supplies cost? Did you have to hire outside help or a model? Does the investment of time result in better quality works? It usually does, as long as too much time isn't wasted along the way.

A trip to the mall may seem like 15 minutes, but in reality it is not. The drive itself might really be 15 minutes, but don't forget the time spent picking up your friends or the time spent waiting for a bus. If you drive you must figure on the time spent driving around the parking lot finding a space. Now allow for the time it takes to walk across the parking lot to the mall and then to the shop you want to visit.

Lesson to be learned: Don't think that a 15-minute trip or errand takes 15 minutes. You will probably be late. Remember, you must figure that there might be traffic or weather that can delay you. It's like the last two minutes of a football or basketball game; technically, yes it's only two minutes. But in reality, with time-outs and different coaching strategies, those 2 minutes might end up being 15 minutes. What if there is an injury or the game goes into overtime? It's the same way with art projects. Outside factors can play a part in the time it takes to complete a project. Sometimes variables out of our control can change the planned outcome. Learn to allow for them. Try to build in some time for insurance, just in case you need it.

Take drawing or painting. In a perfect world the process can flow effortlessly and be a truly spiritual experience. But it is not always that way. What happens if you have a creative block? Do you have a game plan for breaking through the block? Later chapters give you ways to forge through those kinds of problems.

Another lesson to be learned: It doesn't matter what your major—animation, fashion, graphic design, or ceramics—efficient use of studio time is key to your survival. There are many ways to save time in the studio. Talk to your teachers, especially the older ones with more experience.

Even tips related to obsolete methods might be adapted for modern technology. Talk to other students who may have already learned some time-tested techniques passed down from their instructors. Watch and learn from those with experience.

IT MAY SOUND WEIRD AT FIRST

In a materials and techniques class, an instructor once showed me the logic in using her blow-dryer to speed the drying of watercolors. It made sense; I had just never done it before. But I have now. It even works with acrylic paints, although it is important to use the cool setting with acrylics or they will get a strange kind of melted dryness.

Always design on paper first. When you sit at a computer, you should already know what you want to do. Sure, software applications give us tons of tools, including the ultimate gift from the computer gods, the UNDO. Avoid designing on the computer at all costs. The possibilities for change are endless. Sometimes the simplest of drawn lines may be all that is necessary in the design process. Save the heavy equipment for production. This will save time and lead to stronger solutions.

Make four or five 25 percent photocopy reductions of your developed thumbnail sketch, rough comp, or layout. Use these for loose color studies. Markers or color pencils can

12

be applied quickly yielding very effective results. Sometimes doing these small studies can show potential problems that would take much longer to fix in the final stages of a project. You will quickly get the idea of what works and what doesn't work.

GETTING ORGANIZED

Mom always said, "There's a place for everything and everything in its place." Get in the habit of putting stuff away so you'll know where it is when you need it again. It makes sense even if you only find the place once in a while. Keep the items you use frequently closer at hand. Things that aren't used as often can be stored away from the initial work flow. As you set up your work space you will find your own system. Chapter 9 "Setting Up Your Studio" takes a deeper look at this subject.

Besides having an organized work area, try to have an organized calendar whether you use a day planner, a PDA, or a wall calendar. When you get an assignment, put it in your calendar. Put due dates and any checkpoints or other deadlines in your calendar too. While you're at it, put important dates pertaining to school in your calendar. School holidays and breaks, registration week, and finals week should be there too. Put important dates pertaining to your personal life such as birthdays and anniversaries in your calendar too. Look at the congested times, the times when you will be stretched thin. Look at when you will have extra time. Are there any patterns? It is not always easy to work when you have to, especially when creativity must be called upon. Is it available on command?

13

SEEING WITH A FRESH EYE

Each artist works at a different pace. Some artists' work is slow and laborious; others can be quick, pleasant, and painless. At school you will have multiple art projects at the same time. If you have eight hours to work on a project, don't work one eight-hour session. Work eight one-hour sessions. It can be helpful to work each project a little at a time. Each time you return to the project, you will be seeing it with a fresh eye, perhaps picking up on smaller problems or issues before they can become major ones that will cost hours to remedy.

STAY ON TASK

There are many ways to watch your time. We have timers on everything these days. On the oven, the coffee maker, the computer, the television, on phones, even on our watches. That's right, we have timers on our timers. (What does that say about society these days?) Like it or not, you will have to become conscious of time. Be aware that if you vary or drift from your time budget, somewhere else you will have to pay. As they say "you can rob Peter to pay Paul," but it will catch up to you sooner or later. And we will all run out of time eventually.

14

The military teaches how to maximize and use time efficiently through planning, practice, and teamwork. Discipline is key. Remember to set priorities. Get down to work and look at what needs to be finished first, what deadline carries the most weight. This might mean doing something now that you'd rather save for later. Do the most important things with the hottest deadlines first. These priorities can change from day to day, even hour to hour. Some people need help prioritizing successfully.

15

Try the buddy system. Look for someone in need of a partner to keep him or her on task. Maybe it is your roommate, maybe it is a relative, and maybe it is a loved one. It helps to be organized though it is not always easy. Sometimes you need help. Sometimes you can give help. Sometimes it is easier to see the problems or errors in others than it is in ourselves. Look at the people you go to school with or at people you've lived with. Ask yourself the following questions: Who had it together? Who was organized? Who was successful? Learn from what you have seen and whom you have known.

It is important to have downtime when you are not working or thinking about schoolwork. Have a hobby or some outside interest that is not your major. It is helpful to separate work and play.

There is life outside of school. It is the balance of life outside of school with life at school that is important. If there are extracurricular activities, get involved.

17

Extracurricular activities help you become a well-rounded person, and they give a break from schoolwork. These outside activities introduce you to people with different interests and backgrounds. Do not forget about your interests away from school. Be sure to remind yourself from time to time what your priorities are. They may change without you realizing. If they have changed, you should take another look at your calendar. You may have to plan many days, weeks, and even months in advance. Any calendar system you decide to use can help you plan on any level of time as long as you use it. Writing down an appointment is only good if you look at the calendar later to see that you made an appointment.

TIME FOR HOMEWORK

I come from the school of thought that requires two hours of homework for every hour of class time. This is only an estimate. Real times will vary depending on everything else. And everything else will vary for everyone.

Check with your school to see if there might be seminars on time management or counselors that can help you if you have problems with time. Just ask. If you have problems finding someone to help, ask your advisors, teachers, or friends. If they can't help you, ask them if they know someone who can. The worse thing you can do is nothing. Manage time; don't let it manage you.

Half the battle is realizing that time doesn't wait for anyone or anything. Once you accept that fact, you will have made the first step in getting your work done on time. If you allow for unplanned interruptions and a little downtime, you will end up with less stress and stronger projects.

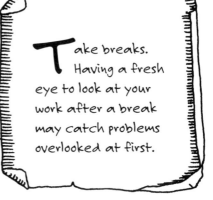

Take breaks. Having a fresh eye to look at your work after a break may catch problems overlooked at first.

NOTES:

19

Great Pyramids of Gizeh, c. 2500 BC

CHAPTER

Keeping It Together

✔ Health: Physical and Mental

✔ Stress

✔ The Bigger Picture

HEALTH: PHYSICAL AND MENTAL

Keeping it together in school is not as easy as it may sound. It might even be chaotic at first. There will be many new people, places, and things introduced to you in a short period of time. Once the dust settles, take a look at your life, both mentally and physically. How are you doing? Be honest with yourself. Do your best to correct any major problems. Address the problems. Do not avoid them. It will be easier to be creative without nagging problems looming in the background. Try to be proactive and not reactive.

One way to do your best work is to be in the best shape both physically and mentally as possible. Unfortunately, this is not always possible. No matter how hard you try, your eating and sleeping habits can be disturbed. While this is not always a bad thing, it can take its toll on you. While in school you should try to experience different things, but not at the cost of your health. You will be meeting many new people from different places. Their eating and sleeping habits or patterns may differ from those that you are accustomed to. What works for one may not work for another. As they say, "Different strokes for different folks."

Physical Health: Care, Nutrition, Exercise, and Sleep

Even if you get enough sleep and eat a balanced diet, sometimes you just can't avoid getting a cold or the flu. You may need a day or two in bed. Sometimes missing one day can save a few days later in the week. Your body will tell you when it needs rest. Listen to it.

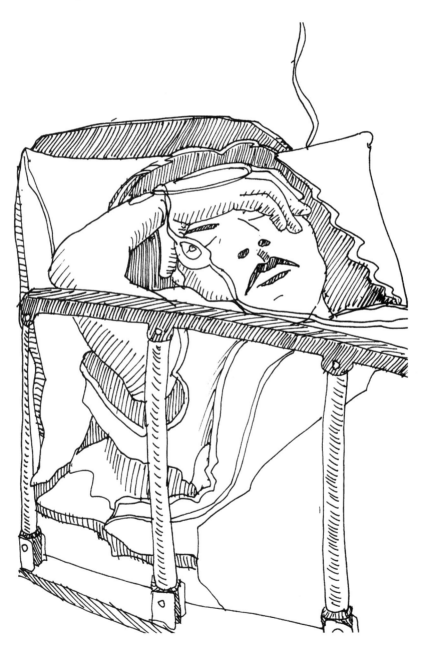

Suppose an illness develops that is more than a cold or suppose an accident happens. Ask yourself the following questions:

- ✔ What if I get sick?
- ✔ Where do I go?
- ✔ Do I have a doctor nearby?
- ✔ Does my school have a health office?
- ✔ Do I need money for the doctor?
- ✔ Do I have money to pay for your visit?
- ✔ Do I know where the closest hospital is?
- ✔ What about dentists and chiropractors?

It is good to find out the answers to these questions before you need them. Have a plan ready. Talk to other students, especially older ones who have been at school for awhile and know the lay of the land. Check with your school: Perhaps there is an infirmary or health office. If not, check at the student center or with your dean of students. Don't forget the yellow pages and the Internet. It doesn't take long. In an emergency would you rather go to a "painless dentist" your friend has been to before or a name in the phone book?

Try to eat well. Sometimes this is easier said than done. How many people really eat well while going to school? If you have a meal plan, use it to your advantage. Many schools now include many of the major fast-food chains as part of the meal package. But try to do the "fast-

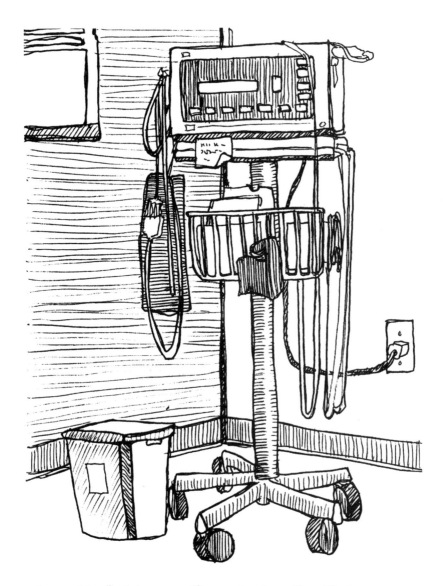

food thing" with care. If you start eating Big Macs or pizza every day, you will probably not be happy with the resulting pounds. Something that often strikes many first-year college students is a condition referred to as the

Eat for your art. Save and recycle your food containers for mixing or storing paint or other supplies. Yogurt containers, milk jugs, and jelly jars all work quite well.

"freshman fifteen." This term refers to fifteen pounds gained during the first year of college, often as a result of poor eating habits. Eating at the wrong times of the day and night, eating junk food, and munching out before bed are good examples of what to avoid. This doesn't mean you can't eat at your favorite fast-food restaurant, just don't do it every day, especially if you are going to go spend the next six hours sitting in the studio.

Your diet and exercise regimen will affect your health. Try to establish or retain good eating and exercise patterns while at school. You do have a say as to what condition your body and mind will be in while at school. You just don't always have total control of it.

When staying awake for extended periods of time to work in the studio, be careful not to overcaffeinate yourself. Some people get jittery, some even get the shakes. For a boost in energy late at night when pulling an all-nighter, try eating a meal. Your body needs fuel to keep working. Watch sugar—its boost is fast but a crash soon follows and you might end up wanting to sleep even more.

Deadlines, class schedules, part-time jobs, commuting time, and budget all play roles in how and when you eat. As stated in the previous chapter, there are only 24 hours in a day. Sometimes dinner from a drive-thru window can free up time to get to the gym or visit a friend. How many people eat in their car while driving? Just look around when you're on the road during the lunch or dinner hours. It's scary and not very safe. Avoid eating while driving.

EATING ON THE RUN

I have a friend who had a really nice Fiat while we were in school. It smelled like french fries. And on rainy days it REALLY smelled like french fries. He ate lunch in his car everyday. Funny how that new car smell can turn into that deep-fried smell. It is the price that has to be paid when you have to do multiple things at the same time. Multitasking is a skill that you should master while in school. You and only you can decide what you are willing to give up. Remember health is important. Don't be too quick to sacrifice it so you have time for TV or shopping. And don't be to quick to eat while driving or for that matter, do anything else while driving. Pull over, take five minutes.

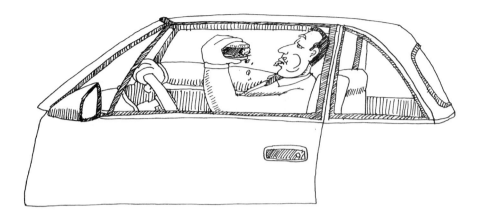

It's easy to get so involved in your work that you hardly ever leave your apartment or studio. The lack of exposure to sunlight can result in the condition referred to as "studio tan," a pale, pasty complexion combined with eyes that are sensitive to sunlight. Try to make a point of getting outside and getting some fresh air. Take a walk, shoot some hoops, throw a Frisbee.

Instead of taking the elevator or escalator, try the steps, even if it is only one or two flights. Try the steps two at a time. Big movement helps the joints, muscles, and cardiovascular system. Anything is better than nothing. People who have a regular workout schedule have more energy. More energy is a good thing. Not only can you get more done, you won't be so tired. Sleep is another factor that plays an important part in your health. The more run-down you are, the more susceptible you will be to colds and flu.

Get to know how much sleep you need to function properly.
Everyone is different. Just because one person can get
by on five hours a night doesn't mean everyone can. Be
sure to get enough for your needs. If you feel tired all
the time, maybe you should see your doctor. It might be
nothing more than a lack of vegetables; then again it
might be a condition requiring medical attention. Get
it checked out. Better be safe than sorry.

If you have a hard time getting up in the morning, make
a deal with a roommate or friend and be each other's
alarm clocks. Give a wake-up call. A ringing telephone
is a very effective way to wake someone. For a
roommate, a squirt gun works wonders.

29

Mental Health: State of Mind, Spiritual Health, and Religion

Are you a religious or spiritual person? Do you get comfort from prayer or going to church or temple? If so, then don't stop just because you are in school. If you are away from your home parish or congregation, find one at or near your school. Some schools have nondenominational services and meetings. Most communities have a number of houses of worship to visit. You don't always have to visit during scheduled services. Many are open all day. Sometimes just sitting quietly in a cathedral or temple can be very restful and soothing. Also remember that you don't need a building to pray, meditate, or reflect. Some people prefer a secluded spot in a natural or peaceful setting. Find what works for you. Don't ignore your spiritual needs. They can play a big part in your mental health and how you deal with life.

Get to know yourself. If medication is in the picture, then be sure to follow your doctor's orders. If you see a therapist, keep your appointments. If you are away from home, see what services your school offers. Avoid situations that have caused problems in the past.

You can be strong most of the time, but sometimes you might just need to vent your frustrations. Try to find positive ways to do this. Some people clean, some paint, some garden. Some people punch walls. Artists' hands are their tools and they don't work well when broken. The everyday pressures that can accompany "doing it right" need to be dealt with or else they will mount up inside until they finally have to come out. When it gets to that point, it is better to control the release of pressure or the

31

results may not be desirable. Don't let the people you love and look to for support and guidance be on the receiving end of an outburst.

STRESS

Schoolwork can cause stress, deadlines can cause stress, relationships can cause stress, work can cause stress, family can cause stress, and self-doubt can cause stress. Life can cause stress. How much should you let it affect you? Can you control it? Maybe you can keep it at a reasonable level.

It is important to have a way to release stress. It can be a physical release such as exercise, dance, riding a bicycle, sports, walking, or punching the heavy bag. It can be a cerebral release such as reading, writing, or listening to music. If praying or meditating helps you cope, then go right ahead. Whatever it is, try to have something that is for you and just for you, something selfish. You can save it for those tense moments or you can make it a part of your everyday life. If you can include a way to relieve or release your tension in your time management plan, you may find your life in school a little less stressful and a little more productive.

Some people eat when they get stressed. While a cheesesteak and fries with a chocolate shake can hit the spot at midnight, they can stay on that spot for years to come. If you are one of those people, at least try to eat healthy. You do not need high blood pressure. You do not need high cholesterol. Try to release stress through a productive exercise or experience and avoid harmful or destructive practices.

THE BIGGER PICTURE

You are about to embark on an excellent journey. Your mind will grow and your experiences will be multiplied. You will meet people who will inspire you, people you will remember for the rest of your life. Being an artistic person, try to think of your education as a starting point and leave yourself open to turns down the road.

Many artists have other creative talents, interests, and gifts. How one looks at a painting and feels its energy can translate into an instrumental arrangement of a musical composition. After years doing the same type of work, sometimes a change can be good. Work evolves. Sometimes we are aware of it. Sometimes we are not. Sometimes it is by our own doing.

34

The people we are, the people we meet, and the experiences we share are all a part of the bigger picture. Life offers many choices. Toil or pleasure? Work or play? You need some of one to appreciate the other. Remember, as a creative person you have a gift that not everyone can appreciate.

Approach your education with an open mind. If you have to work while in school, be realistic about the amount of each you can do successfully. Successfully is a keyword here. Going to school full time, working 40 hours a week, commuting an hour each way, sleeping four hours a night—the result is stress and exhaustion. Do this for three years and maybe earn C's and B's. You don't want to just squeeze by. Doing just enough does not cut it here. What's the point if you can't get work with the portfolio you've compiled? Spread your schooling out. If it takes an extra semester or year to do it right, the time will be worth it. Keep your sanity and create stronger work. Finish strong.

As you get older, your life becomes more complex, and the decisions you make will carry more weight than ever before. Remember you are in school studying art because you love it. Don't lose that passion. Be sensible, have fun, make the most of it. Try to be a realist . . . but not too real. After all, you are an art student.

NOTES:

Stonehenge, c. 2000 BC

CHAPTER

How It's Done and How to Do It

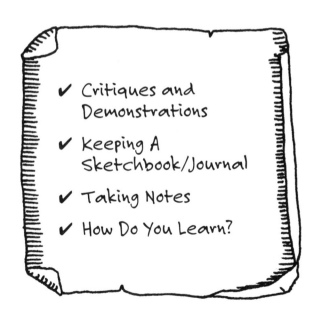

✔ Critiques and
  Demonstrations

✔ Keeping A
  Sketchbook/Journal

✔ Taking Notes

✔ How Do You Learn?

Studying art these days requires that a student be able to learn and absorb information presented in a variety of different formats and environments. As an art student, regardless of studio major, you will be exposed to slide lectures, studio demonstrations, digital media presentations, computer software demonstrations, field trips, internships, lectures, and labs. Not only will you be studying your chosen studio major, but foundation and general education or liberal arts courses as well.

To a student who has never experienced this type of learning, it can be confusing and in some cases overwhelming. Being away from home or on your own for the first time can compound the situation. This is to be an exciting time, an inspirational adventure. To survive and flourish will be a challenge. Studying to be an artist requires talent and discipline. From the basic foundation courses to the most advanced master class, much is taught and learned through critiques and demonstrations. If you are not familiar with the processes, you soon will be.

CRITIQUES AND DEMONSTRATIONS

The critique or "crit" is the process of taking a critical look at a project. How well did your project meet the criteria? How creative was the solution to the problem presented? Was it technically done well? Was it well thought out? The critique session is not meant to break you down, rather show strengths and weaknesses in your work. Do not confuse the critique with an attack on you personally. Crits are designed to help you learn from your mistakes and successes.

As an art student you must grow a thick skin, for your life is to be one of constant critique, whether by clients and art directors or self-inflicted as a method to push technique and expression to new personal highs. Learn to grow from them, and since everyone has an opinion, don't be surprised if one teacher tells you that he likes a part of your work that another teacher thinks you should change. Here is one way to look at it: If one out of five people say something in your work needs to be changed,

41

that might be a matter of personal taste on his or her part, but if four out of five say to change something, it probably needs to be changed. Take notes of your crits and revisit your work addressing those comments.

During the crit, do not apologize for your work. You should not be doing work that you have to apologize for. If you are, you may not be ready for serious studies. During the crit do not defend your work unless asked to. If asked about your work, think about why you made the choices you made. Listen to what is being said. Look at what is being pointed out. There is no need to be upset or get yourself worked up.

Avoid reaching the boiling point. Count to ten. Don't throw anything. No violence. Leave the room. Hold your tongue. Try not to say things that you may regret later.

People place different levels of importance on different parts of a project. One may prefer a simply executed witty idea, while another may lean toward a beautifully rendered piece. Listen to it all. Ask yourself:

42

✔ Did I meet the criteria of the project?

✔ Is this my best work?

✔ Did I give the project enough time?

✔ Did I give the project enough thought?

✔ Did I give the project enough energy?

✔ Can I be proud of my work, my effort?

✔ Did I miss some information given during the assignment?

Answer honestly, even if you are not happy with the answers. If there was a demonstration given, how well you paid attention to it will be evident in your project.

The demonstration or demo is not to be taken lightly. At the demo you will be shown how to do something. Even if you think you know already, pay attention. Like the critique, there can be more than one opinion or way to do something. Depending on how involved the process is, this may be the only time something is shown to you. Position yourself so that you can see and hear what is going on. Be prepared to take notes.

If the demonstration is moving too fast or you do not understand something, say so. If you have to interrupt, apologize. Do not be disrespectful. Be a serious and concerned student. After the demonstration you can ask the instructor if additional support material is available or if another demo is going to be given for another class.

You will take notes at some demos and follow along with others. The demo technique may change with the media or materials. Some will be small intimate groups sitting knee to knee; some will be auditorium-scale projections. Always be prepared to listen and take notes. If you miss the demo, check with the instructor if it will be repeated for another class. Some teachers will let students attend demos for other classes if there is room. Ask. It may be worth the effort.

At the demonstration have an eye for detail. If you miss something, try to leave some room in your notes so that you can come back and fill in the gaps later. Take thorough notes with sketches, captions, arrows, and stars. A good habit to get into is to title and date your notes.

How will you take notes? What will be your vehicle of choice? Will it be a sketchbook, a notebook, a PDA, a laptop computer? As shown in the following list, each has its pros and cons:

	PROS	CONS
Notebook	Affordable	Not archival
	Designed for note taking	Not durable
	Many styles and sizes	Wire binding
Sketchbook	Affordable	Not archival
	Blank pages	Not lined
	Durable	Pages not removable
PDA	Links to computer	Can break
	Portable	Easily misplaced
	Always improving	Limited life span
	Becomes a way of life	Becomes a way of life
Laptop Computer	Powerful	Power limitations
	Software tools available	Digital only
	Portable	Still bulky
	Affordable	Expensive

There are many ways to take notes and there are many devices to take them with. From simple to sophisticated, you should use whatever you are comfortable with as long as it is appropriate for the situation. Doodle, scribble, jot, type, record, point and shoot. Be a low-tech Luddite, a high-tech gadget hound, or something in between. Whichever you choose, try to be consistent but flexible as your choice of tools may change according to the situation.

Regardless of the method, the most important thing is to take notes, take good notes. Take notes that you can read, notes that you can understand. Students who sit through involved multistep, 30-minute demonstrations and take no notes will be the ones with the mistakes and poor projects. Few people have photographic memories; the majority will have to use notes, sketches, photographs, videos, and books for their references. One way to document demos is by keeping and using a sketchbook journal. Its ease of use and portability make it perfect for the classroom, museum, or studio.

Keeping A Sketchbook/Journal

Keeping a chronological sketchbook/journal is like creating your own textbook. In your own words, your daily activities, thoughts, and assignments are recorded for easy reference later. Sometimes a picture _is_ worth a thousand words, so don't be afraid to add diagrams. See what influences your work. Keep your notes together in one place. The notes from lectures, exercises, and demonstrations will all reside here. Mark the words of the inspirational figures in your life, the people who contribute to your growth as an artist. Create this book and then read it. Use it for reference. If you do this you will remember more than you forget. See how your thoughts and ideas develop. Has your point of view changed over time? Has your drawing style?

Choosing Your Sketchbook

Notes are even better when they are read later. One problem that can plague some students is finding the notes taken during a class. Sometimes people take notes but somehow lack the ability to read them later. Avoid taking notes with vine charcoal on newsprint. Although something is better than nothing, charcoal does smear, and 18 X 24-inch newsprint pads were really designed with other uses in mind. It is important to get organized when it comes to taking your notes. Try the ever popular, classic acid-free hardbound sketchbook.

You may already be familiar with the black textured hardcover sketchbook that has become a staple in many artists' studios over the years. They are durable, uniform, archival, and inexpensive. They are available in both horizontal and vertical formats in a variety of sizes. Try to use sizes that are not cumbersome such as $5\frac{1}{2}$ X $8\frac{1}{2}$, $8\frac{1}{2}$ X 11, and 9 X 12 inches. These sizes fit into bags, portfolios, and even pockets. The 11 X 14 size may not look big at first but can end up that way. Try different formats. Maybe your first book is horizontal $8\frac{1}{2}$ X 11, and the second is a vertical $5\frac{1}{2}$ X $8\frac{1}{2}$. You will eventually find the size that is just right for you. If the local art store does not have them in stock, check some of the large bookstore chains in the art book section or by the diaries and journals.

I avoid the wire spiral-bound books. Think of the spiral-bound notebooks you kept through school. How many times did the spring wire binding catch on something and pull away from the paper? Maybe when taking it out of a school bag, the end of the wire catches on the zipper? Next thing you know the wire holding it together has stretched and pulled away from the book. This is the beginning of the end. This book is destined for self-destruction.

Try to avoid having more than one sketchbook going at a time. Even though the idea of one notebook for each subject seems logical, it will force you to carry extra books. Ever grab the wrong book on your way to class? Remember that you probably will also be carrying a portfolio and art supplies or tools of some sort. Get one, use one, and make it a way of life. When it is finished, label it with starting and ending dates, and start another one.

Each book will be chronological, written in the order that things happen. It will contain everything from your notes of a slide lecture on baroque architecture to the phone number of a person that you work with. If you do freelance artwork, client notes may be found here. Work out your ideas for projects; sketch the people around you. Then later when you read the book you have written, you can see the other events that were happening in your life and how they influenced the decisions you made during a project, the colors you chose, the style, even the media.

Studies That Affect Home

I once took a course in graduate school on Vienna and Berlin during the beginning of the 20th century. Both drawings and notes on how art and music were affected by the politics and social morality of the time filled my sketchbook. The pages following the lecture notes were full of my sketches for the renovation of a rowhouse my wife and I were working on at the same time.

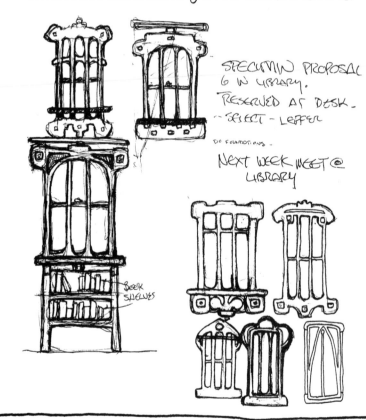

SPECIMIN PROPOSAL
6 IN LIBRARY.
RESERVED AT DESK.
- SELECT - LETTER

DO FOUNDATIONS -

NEXT WEEK MEET @ LIBRARY

BOOK SHELVES

The sketches of the house interior and exterior were heavily infused with art nouveau and Wiener Werkstatte references, large murals, and a small outdoor rose garden. Many of the ideas inspired by the works of Gustav Klimt and Alphonse Mucha never made it beyond the pages of the sketchbook, but they did inspire other ideas that came to fruition in the house.

Choosing Your Writing and Drawing Tools

The composition or makeup of your book will depend on you and the direction you follow while studying art. Don't be afraid to experiment with different media in your book, but please be aware of what you use and how it may affect the rest of the book. You may like to write with one type of pen and draw with another. Maybe you prefer

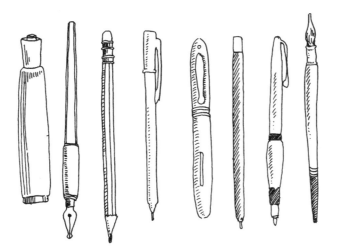

pencils for writing and markers or watercolors for sketching. It's up to you.

Finding a writing or drawing tool that you are comfortable with may take some time. If a friend has a pencil or pen you have never used before, ask if you may try it. Make a few strokes with it, write a few words with it. There are so many different pens to choose from. Some are expensive, some are disposable. How does it flow? Does it have a comfortable grip?

Remember that some ink will bleed through the page. Markers may bleed through a page and even onto the next page, making it difficult to read any writing you may have or want to put there. Watercolors when dry may wrinkle the page. A fountain pen with black water-based ink allows the addition of gray washes by taking a wet brush to the ink lines. But care must be taken when using other water-based media with it. If you choose to use a fine-point marker, try to get one with permanent ink. If you choose ballpoint pen (great for line and shading), be aware that different manufacturers' black ink can vary greatly from warm to cool. Gel pens write smooth but seem to smudge. If you are left-handed, smudging and smearing may be an issue because you will be writing from left to right and your hand will be rubbing against the letters and lines you have just placed on the page. If you use a pen, it should be one with fast-drying ink.

If you use pencils, be careful not to choose graphite that is too hard. A 4H pencil holds its point for a long time between sharpenings but produces a lighter line than an HB. Just the slightest rubbing together of pages when flipping through a book can smear pencil marks, leaving already faint lines a challenge to read.

Your sketchbook may end up being filled with a variety of media. Paint, pencil, photographs, tape, glue, ink, rubbings, crayons. It's all good. Just remember that you want to be able to revisit this book later and be able to understand what you drew and wrote. Once you find the instrument you like to write and draw with, start refining your search. Just walk down the aisles of an art or office supply store and you will find miles of pens and pencils. Good luck in your quest for the perfect drawing and writing tool.

Starting Your Sketchbook

Your sketchbook is a very personal thing and you will find your own formula for it as your work develops it. Each book that you keep will be better than the one before it. Each succeeding book will be a little more organized, with better drawings and more interesting information. You should feel free to follow your own artistic vision. The following is my formula for a sketchbook. It is supplied as a guide or a point of departure.

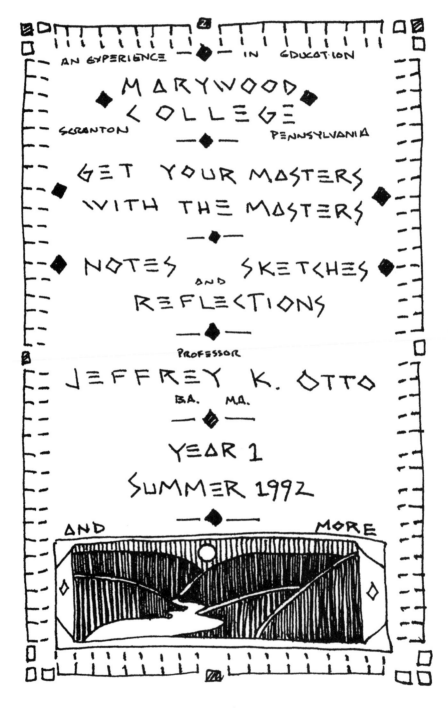

AN EXPERIENCE — IN EDUCATION

MARYWOOD COLLEGE

SCRANTON — PENNSYLVANIA

GET YOUR MASTERS WITH THE MASTERS

NOTES AND SKETCHES REFLECTIONS

PROFESSOR

JEFFREY K. OTTO

B.A.   M.A.

YEAR 1

SUMMER 1992

AND   MORE

The first page should be left blank. This is a buffer page that protects your title page. The second right-hand page will be the title page. This page should have your name and the contact information you may want to add in case you lose your book—phone number, e-mail address, mailing address, that is up to you. It should also contain the date the book was started. You can even leave a space for the date when it was finished (to be filled in at completion of the book). I like to make this page an illustrated title page. It will be revisited many times as I work on the illustration. I begin the body of the book on the next right-hand page, not using the back of the title page.

I prefer printing and drawing with ink on paper. It doesn't smudge. It encourages me to be confident and sure of my marks and comments. But I always leave white space for notes later. For while I may be sure of myself at the time I am writing or sketching, I may learn something later that changes my mind or point of view. I may learn something that further supports my original thoughts and I want to add to it.

Set aside an area (I use the last 2 pages) in the book for names, numbers, and addresses of people that you meet and work with. It's much easier than searching through the body of the book later looking for a number. When I finish a sketchbook, I transfer the names and numbers into my address book. Years later it is interesting to look back at the people you associated with during that time of your life.

THIS BOOK
CONTAINS THE SKETCHES
AND IDEAS OF THE
ARTIST JEFFREY K. OTTO.

STARTED IN
HISTORIC WILLIAMSBURG, VA
ON JUNE 25, 2001 WHILE
AWAY ON VACATION AT
GREENSPRINGS PLANTATION

IF FOUND PLEASE
RETURN TO:

JEFFREY K. OTTO
911 SOUTH GLENWICK RD.
KESBURG PENNSYLVANIA
18903

Take Care of Your Book

Keeping a single book with all of your notes and drawings in it can help simplify and organize. But what happens if it gets damaged or worse yet, you lose it? Realize that by putting all your eggs in one basket, you risk losing all of them. The sketchbook must become a part of you, a part of your life as an artist. My sketchbook (5½ x 8½) is always in my bag. I take it everywhere all the time, from concert halls and museums to nightclubs and subway stations. My sketchbooks contain drawings of Babatunde Olatunji in concert, ruins of the cathedral in San Galgano, Gunther Herbig conducting the Philadelphia Orchestra, even anxious commuters waiting in Penn Station.

57

In the past 20 years of keeping sketchbooks, I have never lost a single one. Recently I "backed them up." I bookmarked the really important pages (there were many more than I thought there would be) and photocopied them. Some of them required some additional care and repair.

Bookbinding tape helped the spine of a few books. There was another that I had repaired about 10 years ago with duct tape. Never tear pages out of your book. Doing so can affect the binding, because the pages are usually sewn together in sections or signatures. Torn pages should be repaired as soon as you discover them. You can use transparent tape, white linen framing tape, or even masking tape. You can be as archival as you choose. The paper is probably acid free, as many sketchbooks are these days. Try to keep them in good repair and you will be able to use them for years to come.

Your sketchbook will fill rapidly if you use it daily. Since it is chronological, it will contain not only demo and lecture notes, but sketches and business notes as well. A smaller size sketchbook fits in portfolios and backpacks. All notes regarding any project are made there. Taking notes for a client meeting is much like taking notes for a project in a class. Again always start with a date and a name on a new right-hand page.

Be cautious about what you draw and write in the sketchbook. This living document is about you; don't enter things that you might regret or be embarrassed by later. Use common sense. Some instructors will require you to keep a sketchbook and ask to see it at midterms and finals. Don't shoot yourself in the foot. There was a show

* GUNTHER HERBIG *
CONDUCTOR

JULY 17, 1986

60

of Leonardo DaVinci's sketchbook pages in New York City. Imagine if there were lewd sketches drawn next to one of his great invention ideas—a sketch of a helicopter with a dirty joke written next to it. Use good judgment.

Do not waste pages. If you draw a picture you don't like, try to fix it, or use the page for other information. As a teacher, I have seen books with page after page of wasted paper. Do not tear pages out of your book. That will only compromise the integrity of the binding. Remember that this sketchbook should hold the place of an important volume or document in your library. It represents much time and energy. It is a valuable resource and should be treated that way.

TAKING NOTES

First of all, write or print legibly. If you cannot read your own notes then what is the point? Many artists develop a calligraphic style or flare to their printing or writing. Have you ever looked at an architect's handwriting or printing? Have you ever looked at your doctor's? Which would you rather read? Taking notes can be a work of art in itself. The process can be a study in typography and design. Longhand or hand printing, develop your own style.

When taking notes, the heading or main subject should be in larger and/or bolder letters. You may even underline it or place a star to the left of the subject heading (I reserve stars for the second time I read notes using them as reminders of important things). Then move to a new line and start writing the main facts as they are given. Try to leave breathing room between lines or next to

61

paragraphs in case there is information given later about that topic. It is easier to have all the information in one place. Be sure to include diagrams and sketches.

A picture is worth a lot of words, maybe even a thousand. Sometimes it is more economical to draw something than it is to write about it. Sometimes a little of both works. Do not forget punctuation marks and other symbols. & = and; $ = dollars, cost, or money; > = greater than or bigger than; < = less than or smaller than; @ = at. Use whatever you are comfortable with.

62

You will constantly be refining your note-taking skills. Find the combination that works for you. Be concise and to the point. When taking notes, be sure to grasp the essence or main theme of the information. Like an outline, start with the main topic, and then add the defining details as you fill in the gaps. Key words and doodles can be enough to trigger your memory. If later you cannot fill the gaps yourself, compare notes with a friend or classmate. They may have some gaps in their notes that also need filling.

Compare and share the knowledge. You will have your own take on the information being presented to you, but that is just one point of view. Have you ever worked with a study partner or in a study group? Another student might hear the same lecture and get something a little different out of it, maybe something that you never thought of. Having someone to share and compare that information with can be helpful and enlightening, if you choose the right person.

Some teachers will set up study groups for their classes. Look around you, start your own. Do you have friends in the class? Are they the hard workers? Be careful whom you select. Look for the smart people, the talented ones who do the best work. The people who have positive things to contribute. Look around you. Who is doing the work you wish you were doing? That is who you want to pair up with or be in a study group with. The class clown is funny, the bohemian is offbeat, and the slacker is . . . well the slacker is a slacker.

These people are all part of the mix. They make art school interesting and colorful. You can learn from them all. It is important to position yourself with the people who can inspire you to do your best. Don't sit in the back of the room with the clowns, get a good seat up front so you don't miss a thing.

The Slide Lecture

It is often difficult to take notes in slide lectures. The room is dark and it is hard to see the page in front of you. How does one take notes in the dark? One solution is to sit close to the screen. The light reflected off of it can be enough to illuminate your page. It also helps to be up close when looking at details or specific areas of the projected image. Another solution is to use a small reading light, the type that clamps onto the book for reading in bed. They are reasonably priced and might be a good investment if your curriculum or course of study contains many art history courses.

When taking notes at a slide lecture, start on a new right-hand page of your sketchbook. Put the date at the top, the instructor's name, and the course name. This will make it easier to find your notes later. It also creates a document of your attendance in the class. Next imagine or lightly draw lines dividing your page so you can fit four to six slide drawings on the right-hand side, leaving room for notes on the left side.

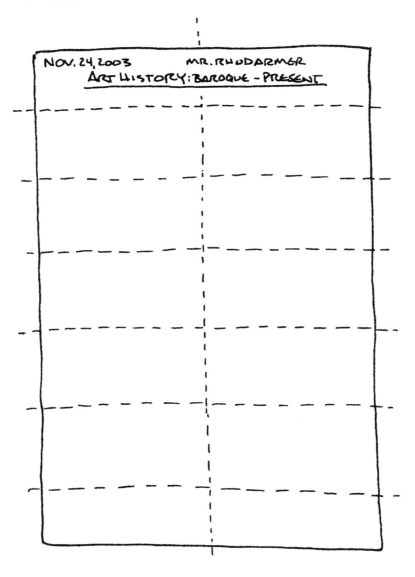

NOV. 24, 2003   MR. RHODARMER
ART HISTORY: BAROQUE - PRESENT

65

Slide lectures usually have an order or sequence, presented by time period or by artist. Start with a heading on the top left side of the page. The heading might be the name of the period or style of art. Below that place a number one (1) on the left side followed by the title of the work or the artist name. Include any dates given. Then next to it on the right-hand side of the page, draw a box for the sketch of the slide. Start with the format of the piece—vertical or horizontal. Place a number one (1) next to it that will correspond with the number of the title on the left. Then as you listen to the facts about the work being shown, sketch it in the box. You won't have a great deal of time for details; just be sure to capture the essence of the piece. Add shadows if needed. Use arrows to point out areas of importance. While sketching continue to jot notes on the left. When the slide changes, leave a space for one more line of writing and begin your next heading. Place a number two (2) on the left side of the page and add the title, artist, and date of the next slide. When that slide is shown, draw a box on the right side in the proper format and sketch that work of art. Place a number two (2) next to that drawing. Now repeat the process, filling in words and sketching as you listen.

Some instructors provide a handout with a listing of slides and additional information. As soon as you get it, date it and put your name on it. It should be kept with your notebook. Some students staple these handouts to pages in their sketchbooks. I remember a professor who didn't want his students to take notes during his slide lectures. He wanted undivided attention. He didn't want anyone to miss anything that he was talking about. He supplied

NOV. 24, 2003   DR. RHODARMER
ART HISTORY: BAROQUE – PRESENT

REMBRANDT VAN RIJN
_____ __ _____ _____ _____.
_____ ____ ____ ____ __ __ __. .

1. SYNDICS OF THE
   CLOTH GUILD.
   1662 ___ ____ ___
   ____ ____ __ __ __

1.

2. SELF PORTRAIT
   1659
   ____ _____ _____ _____
   ___ ___ _____ __ ____

2.

3.

3.

the class with a handout listing names, titles, and dates.
Remember, your sketches do not take the place of
written notes; they are part of the written notes. They
all are part of the note-taking process.

67

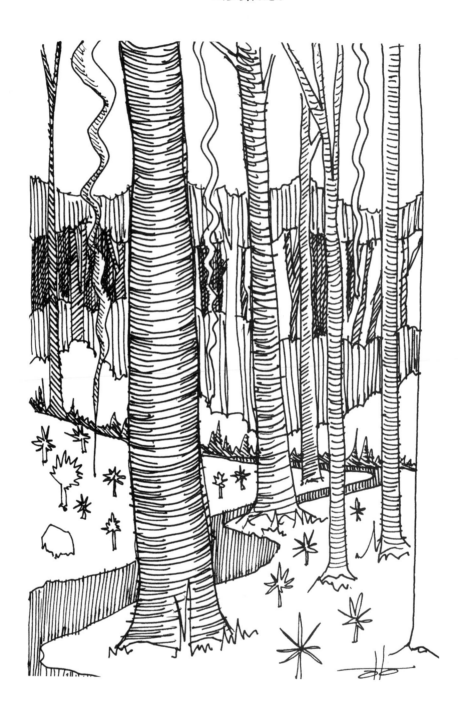

The Studio Demo

Taking notes of a studio demo is similar to taking notes of a slide lecture. It requires you to take a combination of notes and draw sketches. Depending on the studio, it can be a little awkward. How do you get comfortable to take notes gathered around a potter's wheel or a glass furnace? Its not always possible and sometimes you will have to adjust your position to get close enough to see, or to get situated so you can write.

One way to practice is to draw in a small sketchbook while standing up. Whether standing in the woods or on a train platform, get comfortable and draw. A larger sketchbook becomes more of a challenge to handle. If you position yourself close to the subject area, then run out of ink or break a point, what will you do? Make sure you have an extra pen or pencil when the demo starts.

Again, begin with a fresh right-hand page and date the top, adding the name of the class and instructor. Depending on the demo, you may need to divide your page into sections. Because the demonstration will more than likely be presented in a step-by-step fashion, it should be easy to follow. Studio demos are usually in a sequential format. Number the steps. Use bold letters, caps, or underlines to signify important steps or new processes. Draw sketches of the actual piece being created during the demo to help trigger memories later.

I suggest taking the slide lecture approach and use boxes to the right for your sketches and notes to the left. Try to leave the left page blank so later you can add steps or details that you may have missed. Do not be afraid to ask questions. Chances are you will not be the only person with a question. Someone else may ask a question that you have.

If the instruction is not clear and you are not getting the point, you may ask another student later when the demo is finished so as not to interrupt the presentation. Again, you can always ask the instructor if another demo will be given to another class and if you can attend it.

If you are taking notes in a painting studio, are you planning to paint in your sketchbook? If you are, are you using a paint medium that will dry quickly and not cause pages to stick together? Some students and artists don't mind their sketchbooks having wrinkled, water-warped pages, as long as the information they want is translated on the pages. I have seen some very wrinkled, tattered, patched, and battered sketchbooks. Sometimes it is better to just take notes with words and drawings, and sometimes you may want to follow the demo using the same materials as the instructor. How you do it will vary depending on your major, space, instructor, and medium.

The Computer Software Demonstration

Digital media and presentation techniques are changing so rapidly that note taking as you know it could change before your very eyes. The change may not alleviate the need for note taking, just the manner in which it is done. Learning software requires understanding what the software application is intended to do.

Some instructors start by giving an overview and show what the entire application is capable of, then go back

70

and deliver smaller lessons isolating specific tools or groups of related functions. This will vary with the application you are learning. Software that is fairly new has historically had a lower version number with the title. A higher number usually indicates that there have been many updates and improvements to a piece of software since its initial release. Photoshop 2.5 for instance offered more tools and functions than Photoshop 2.0, but not nearly as many as Photoshop 7. Now major software manufacturers are adding letters like CS to the software titles. If you are not sure what version you are learning or using, be sure to ask your instructor.

If the demonstration is a projection of the instructor's workstation screen accompanied by her narration, give her your attention. If you cannot see, ask if you can reposition yourself to get a better view. This also goes for audio as well as visual. If you cannot hear, ask to move closer to the source. Twenty computers running in a quiet room can still be quite noisy.

If the teacher instructs you to turn off your monitor, then do so. Do not surf the net or do your homework for another class, pay attention. Even if you think you already know the software, watch and listen. There is often more than one way to accomplish something with a piece of software and there are many power user tips to learn. Some software applications are more intuitive or easy to use than others. You will have to take time to explore and experiment. That is part of the learning process. When taking notes, don't be afraid to group things together in families and draw circles around them, using arrows to show how and where they relate.

71

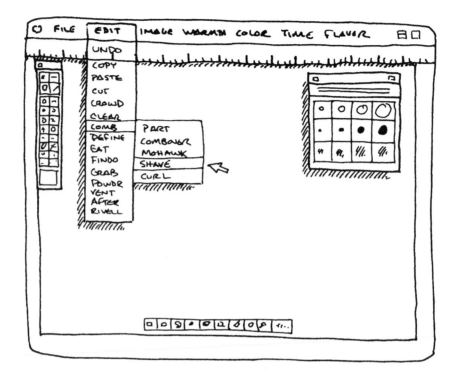

If you have time before the demo, look at all of the pull-down menus and check for familiar processes and commands. Look at the hierarchy of the application. Almost every program requires a new project to be started and named. The process of "file > new, save as > name" is pretty standard. This can be noted by drawing a down and to the right L-shaped arrow underneath the word FILE pointing to the word NEW. This indicates that NEW is the next sublevel of the FILE menu hierarchy, much like indenting while writing an outline. If you break it down to basics, the teaching and learning of computer software applications is not much different from teaching and learning any other process with multiple options. It is not rocket surgery.

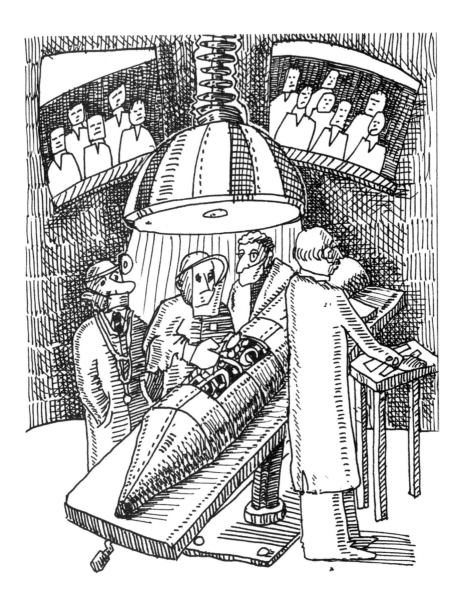

I recommend spending more time watching what is being shown to you. Only follow along on your computer if the instructor tells you to. There are many books, CDs, DVDs, videos, and Web sites where a rerun of the demo or

73

When writing down assignment or job specs, always remember to ask vertical or horizontal format/orientation when writing down measurements. Also ask if there is a template or spec sheet to work from.

refresher material can be found. Pay attention to what your instructor is pointing out. Also remember that computers and software are just tools. They can be powerful tools or they can be wasted tools. By paying attention during demos you will be learning the proper way to use those tools. Use them wisely.

BUT DID YOU SIGN A CONTRACT?

With digital technology changing the way research and term papers are written, you should be well versed in the ownership of intellectual property. Portions of creative works are "sampled" and turned into something new. People are downloading illegal copies of music, software, even movies, and the artists who created them are seeing nothing for their efforts. Keeping track of your rights and responsibilities regarding copyright laws is crucial in our sue-happy society.

Plagiarism or copying without permission and claiming authorship is an offense that carries the penalty of expulsion from most schools. If you get caught and are lucky enough not to be kicked out of school, you will have a reputation among the faculty and their trust may be gone forever.

What about copyrights, work for hire, licensing, contracts, work on spec? What do you know about these? Do yourself a favor and start learning today. There are many books regarding these issues. Look for books that are directly geared toward the arts. Professional organizations such as the Graphic Artists Guild have published excellent books to help guide artists through the jungle of legal jargon that makes the facts difficult to understand. Visit your library, talk to your advisors, get straight with this and play by the rules. You don't even want to mess around here.

How Do You Learn?

Liberal arts or general education courses, computer software demonstrations, slide lectures, and studio classes all require different note-taking and study skills. It is important for you to be aware of how and when you learn best. I prefer to attend lectures and write in the morning and do studio work in the afternoons and evenings. The time of day or night that you plan for work, study, or play is not always something that you can control. Certain classes may only be offered early in the morning. If it is a prerequisite for another course, your decision to take it when it is offered later in the day may affect your graduation date. Even if you might do better if it were offered at a different time, sometimes you just have to deal with it. Would you turn down a job offer after graduation because work starts at eight in the morning? Be prepared to adjust your physical clock as well as your alarm clock.

Some students do well with linear presentations of information while others find a nonlinear approach more suitable to their ways of gathering and holding information. Think of linear as a sequential step-by-step way of presenting and learning and nonlinear as parts of information, lots of parts that can be used together.

Linear Learning

We learn the letters of the alphabet: a b c d e f g h i j in a specific order. Once we learn the letters, we learn the vowels: a e i o u, and then the consonants: b c d f g h j k l and so on. Next we are taught that words are made

76

from combinations of the letters, and that all words require at least one vowel. We start with simple one-syllable words such as "cat," move on to two-syllable words such as "tiger," then move on to three-syllable words such as "sabertooth," and so on. Next we start thinking about sentences. For the purpose of this chapter, we will call this linear learning and teaching: learning the information in a sequential or constructive order.

Nonlinear Learning

A nonlinear approach to the same information might be, "The Alphabet: for written communication we use symbols that represent sounds. Different combinations are used to make up words, sentences, then paragraphs, and so on."

An example would be "The dog ate the cat." Here we have a sentence made up of five words each containing three letters. Each word is one syllable, and each contains at least one vowel. The vowels are the letters i u e a o. There are long sounds and short sounds to the vowels. The "a" in the word "cat" sounds like "ahhh". The "a" in the word "ate" sounds like the letter "a." There are also consonants that can have both hard and soft sounds such as "c" and "g."

Here we have two ways of presenting the same basic information. Some people can grasp the nonlinear approach and some cannot. In the United States most children are taught their ABCs sequentially through nursery rhymes and songs. Art can be similar.

When teaching studio methods, some instructors favor a sequential step-by-step tutorial approach to teaching, while others prefer to break the same information down into components introducing a little of each part at a time. I have found through observing students and teachers alike that when a student realizes how she learns and can team with a faculty member who teaches in that fashion, she will enjoy learning with fewer struggles. Unfortunately, this is not always possible, especially in smaller art departments where there might only be one person to teach a particular course or subject area. Do the best you can, be aware of how you learn, when you are most creative, and what types of instructors you work well with.

If you have never taken a course with an instructor, it may take you a few lectures or demos to get a handle on how that instructor teaches. Once you get the hang of it, the lessons will be easier to follow. When you have had the same instructor in a previous course, you will have a clue as to the methodology that the instructor will use to pass on information.

Some instructors may go off on tangents and you may find it hard to follow; others have a strong game plan that is easy to follow. Either way you must get the information. It is your responsibility to yourself. Remember, as a student you should be a sponge for knowledge and information. Absorb as much as possible.

Get Out the Dictionary

I once had an instructor in a graduate education course whose vocabulary and command of the English language were so advanced to mine that I had to use the dictionary to figure out what exactly his lecture was about. While it was still fresh in my mind, I would then rewrite the notes in my own words. I got the information, but it took work. I never would have survived the course if I worked only from the original lecture notes. Rewriting notes is a great way to study. Rewrite and organize, highlight and edit. Each time you do this, you will remember more.

There are many ways of organizing your notes. Half of this chapter was written on a handheld PDA and a portable keyboard. This is a very portable way to create and keep files that can be transferred to and from a computer. But like all technology these days, it is ever changing. Some people prefer standard school composition books or even loose-leaf notebooks; some (like myself) prefer to keep ongoing sketchbook journals that combine sketches and notes. Some people even dictate into a small audio recording device.

Getting organized from the beginning is a good idea. Have a place to work that is separate from where you eat and prepare food. Have a place to store your work and important school papers. It may eventually morph into something more akin to chaos, but try to have a basic guideline to follow or return to when things go awry or when a new project or semester is about to begin.

Studying art should be a challenging and rewarding adventure. Take your studies seriously. You don't have to go to the biggest or best-known art school to get a good education. You will only get out of school what you are willing to put into it. Make the most of it. After all you are paying for it with years of your life.

Use Spellcheck!

NOTES:

Snake Goddess, Knossos c. 1600 BC

CHAPTER

4

Relationships with Peers, Faculty, and Advisors

- ✔ Responsibility
- ✔ Taking Advice
- ✔ Don't Be Afraid to Ask Questions
- ✔ Following the Chain of Command
- ✔ Experiencing Life with Others
- ✔ Positioning Yourself
- ✔ Networking

83

Establishing solid and positive relationships with your peers, faculty, and advisors is one of the first things you should do and one of the best things you can do when you get to school. Get to know your advisors and teachers. Get to know your peers. Look around you in class. Do you recognize anyone? Even if it's only from a brief orientation meeting, there is a certain comfort in recognizing a face. A chance encounter may be all it takes to establish a lifelong friendship. But still, use good

judgment in who you choose to be associated with. Many of the people you meet from here on in will be people pursuing the same career goals as you. As time goes by, you will all grow creatively and professionally. You never know when you may be in a position of need or to hire or help someone. Isn't it good to have an old friend or associate to call on? Make good choices and good friendships. Even if you only touch base once a year, being thought of in a good light is key.

RESPONSIBILITY

Some days are good days; some days are bad days. Some days it feels like you're on top of the world. Some days the weight of the world is resting on your shoulders. All and any of these days will affect you in both positive and negative ways. As a result, you will make good decisions and you will make not-so-good decisions. No matter what decision you make, you should be ready and able to take responsibility for it. If you make a mistake and learn from it, then it can be looked at as a productive mistake. But if you make a mistake and push blame on someone or something else or shrug responsibility, it will be looked at as a negative mistake. You will probably not learn from it. You may even repeat the same mistake. It won't be a growth experience, just a narrow escape that causes anxiety and grief for you and possibly others.

If the conditions you are under when you make important decisions are less than ideal, you may not always think things through. Try not to paint yourself into a corner. If you can find some time to think things over or consult others who may be helpful in your decision making, do so.

85

You may know someone who has had an experience similar to what you are facing. How did he do? Was his outcome successful? Was it a positive experience? Or did he fall on his face? You can learn from either one.

Try to think things out thoroughly before you commit. You can state that in your opinion, based on what you know at a certain time, you believe that you made the proper choice. If you mess up, take responsibility. Part of the experience of learning is learning from one's mistakes. Try not to put yourself in the same position again. You will be respected more by admitting that you did something wrong and learning from it than giving some lame excuse.

DON'T MAKE EXCUSES

There are six hundred students in my department and a few times each year a number of students fail out of school. These students usually have not been able to keep up their grades or do satisfactory work. Some of them have done good work and are very talented but are inconsistent and drop or fail as many courses as they pass. In other cases they are good students who have had life throw them a curve. A death in the family, children, a divorce, a roommate with similar problems, any can cause a good student to have a bad session. Returning to school while the same problems are occurring can be deadly to an academic record. There is an appeal process they can go through to try and get readmitted into school.

One of the most important factors we look for is

someone who takes responsibility for what has happened. The person who says "I messed up, I wasted too much time" or " I've been partying too much" has more of a

shot at getting back into school than the person who gives the old "the dog ate my homework" or "the teacher didn't like me" excuse.

TAKING ADVICE

The job of your faculty and staff are to prepare you to enter the workplace. Many of them are also working professionally in the field while teaching. Many of them spent years in the field before teaching and are now sharing their experience and knowledge. Some will be fresh out of grad school; some will be ready to retire. Each has a point of view or perspective to share. Each has an experience, a story to tell.

For the next few years, you have advisors available to help you think out some very important decisions if you choose to use them. They are there for you. After you are out of school, you may find occasion that you wish you still had that support. You may even call an old professor looking for some direction. Advice can come in many forms. A story about an old student or even a personal experience can shed light on an outcome overlooked by the student. Even something as simple as a positive upbeat attitude may give that extra push needed to come to a decision.

To Use Advice or Not Use It

It is your responsibility if and how you will use the advice that you are given. I am reminded of the age-old cartoon and movie skit with the hero trying to make a decision and the devil appears on one shoulder and an angel appears on the other. You see advice is not always good. It also depends on what your definition of good might be. The choice you make may have long-lasting consequences.

88

When taking advice, it is good to take note of who you are taking advice from. If you ever need to explain yourself, it is better to be able to quote a source of information than it is to say, "somebody told me. . . ." This is not passing the buck if you are acting on information you are led to believe credible and not confidential.

Get to know your instructors and advisors. The better you know them, the better idea you will have as to who might be the best person to ask for advice. The better they know you and your situation, the better they will be able to help you. Take the advice of your advisors. Then decide on how you will use that advice. Remember it's their job to help you survive and succeed in school. The better you know one another, the easier it will be.

89

Don't Be Afraid to Ask Questions

Don't be afraid to ask questions. If you don't have all of the information needed to complete a successful assignment, you need to get it. Keep in mind that there is a time and place for everything. By all means ask if you need to if the opportunity for questions presents itself. You may have to wait until a later time. Your instructors may have office hours or another way to contact them. Don't procrastinate. Ask respectfully; remember you're seeking information. You may have a question that is not regarding an assignment. It may be something more personal. You may need to see a counselor. If you don't have an advisor, approach a teacher or your department head. One of them should be able to guide you to the help you seek. Once you get the answer to your question, remember it, write it down if you have to. Instructors are there to help, but they do get annoyed when they answer the same question over and over again.

If your questions are regarding your curriculum or academic progress, be sure to see someone at the school, someone who works there and has access to accurate and official information. While a friend might have a clue as to her particular situation, she may not know all about yours. Her advice may be given with good intentions, but that's not going to carry any weight if you suddenly are short 3 credits

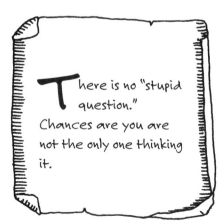

There is no "stupid question." Chances are you are not the only one thinking it.

to graduate. "My friend told me to take those classes" is not a valid excuse in such an important situation. In some schools, you may have little choice as to your classes or even schedules. Follow the path laid out for you. There is a reason for course prerequisites and following them.

Following the Chain of Command

As you seek advice or answers, it is important to address the proper people. Follow the chain of command. This means to start with the people closest to you who know of the situation you are speaking of or can help. If it is a matter of questioning a grade given by an instructor on a class project, do not go to the president or dean. Talk to that instructor. After all, she is the person who gave the grade. Do not approach her with an attitude. That is the quickest way to get shut down. Talk to her seeking enlightenment. You may need to make an appointment to see that person when she can give your matter complete attention. Do not stop her as she enters class or is on her way to catch a train.

If the issue is a more serious classroom-related problem, you should still start with the teacher. Think about what it is you want. Is it an explanation, clarification, an apology? Do not be too quick to judge until you get as much information as possible. Try to put yourself in his position. Get both sides of the story. Would you make the same decision? Maybe you would, maybe you would not.

If you still feel the issue has not been resolved or explained, then go to your department chairperson, the next in the chain of command. The chain is set in order

of responsibility. First the instructor, who is responsible for the class. Next the chairperson, who is responsible for all of the instructors and all of the classes in the department. The assistant dean or the dean would be next. They are responsible for all of the departments. Approaching people of authority beyond the dean—the vice presidents, president, and provost—are rarely appropriate or necessary.

Even if your school does not have this many levels of administration, rarely will you ever have an issue that will require you to go to the president. Start locally and only work up the ladder as and if absolutely necessary. If every student issue went to the president, the school would stop running. Try to resolve your school-related problems and issues without involving the entire administration. But, if the situation is something that a school official should be aware of, then you should make him aware of it without understating or exaggerating.

EXPERIENCING LIFE WITH OTHERS

Living and working with new and different people can add much to your school experience as well as your own personal growth. The more diverse the peer group, the more diverse the experience. People from different cultures or backgrounds may look at things with a different level of importance than you might. Different ethnic or regional foods can add an enjoyable and flavorful twist to school.

If you are not sure of how to do something at school, ask a friend or a classmate. The advice of your peers can be very helpful. Again, remember to consider the source when taking that advice. Does that person have more experience or better success than you do? Is that person extreme in his own actions? Is he respected for what he is doing?

At school a common interest will bring together people from diverse backgrounds. You may also find that a common background will bring together people of diverse academic interests. People sharing who they are and

94

what they know is one of the great parts of being in school. If you are only experiencing the classroom aspect of school, you are missing out on a lot. Think about it. Not all education takes place in the classroom. The maturation process of you the artist also affects you the person.

POSITIONING YOURSELF

Do not be a loner. You'll miss out on some great experiences. Try to position yourself with people who are positive and have a clue. People with a goal and the drive to get there. They don't have to be people like you, just people with a purpose. This is not a popularity contest. You don't have to be best friends with anyone, just be aware of who has got it together. You may know them from a club. You may simply be in class together. People from different backgrounds have new things to offer. Yes, the class clown is funny, the bohemian type is cool, and the international exchange student is exotic. Any or all of them can make learning a fun and enjoyable experience. Look for the people who do the very best work and are having fun while doing it. A strong work ethic will get you farther than laziness any day of the week.

When you look at successful people, you should ask yourself "what is their definition of success?" Then ask yourself, what is _my_ definition of success? Why are those people successful? How are they successful? How do they conduct themselves in public, how do they speak? Do they dress, eat, or study differently? If you cannot put your finger on it, maybe it is simply a state of mind. Look for shortcomings as well. What is lacking in their lives?

95

96

Everything usually comes at a price. Is there something you are willing to give up to get something else? Some folks think that the grass is always greener on the other side of the fence. Sometimes it is, sometimes it is not. Try to associate with people who can have a positive affect on you.

NETWORKING

When I was in college I was an idealistic artist, for that matter a very idealistic person. I remember my mother saying "It's not what you know, it's who you know." I remember always fighting her on that. I figured if you knew the right stuff, then that would be enough to ensure success. I eventually realized that mom was partially right. What good is knowing the right stuff if no one knows you know the right stuff? So many years later I have adapted that saying and adopted it in my teachings. "It's not what you know or who you know, it's who you know knows you know what you know." Think about it!

Think about the people you knew or remember from another time or place in your life. Now, of those people, who are you thinking good things about and who do you have not so good thoughts for? Now suppose you were in a position to help one of these people. Maybe by offering a job, or sharing some wealth, or even voting for in an election. Who are you going to help? Exactly, the person that brings the positive thought to mind. Try to make a good impression on the people you meet. You never know when you may need to call on them. You never know when they may need to call on you.

Suppose that ten years from now you are an art director. You need to hire a freelancer for something. You look into your address book and you see the names of people who are capable of doing the job. But one of those names is someone associated with a negative energy. Maybe a fight, maybe they jammed you up on a previous job, or just maybe they have an attitude that is not worth the time to deal with. Who are you going to call? Try to make a good impression on the people you work with.

Share the knowledge of who you know with others. When seeking information, if the person you have contacted cannot help, ask them if they know someone who can. Likewise, if someone contacts you looking for some information and you don't have it, try to pass on a name of someone who might. It is great when you can help. Please think twice about casually giving out someone's confidential contact information. Handing out an unlisted telephone number without permission might cost you a good contact. Use good judgement. Do your best to never leave a bad impression.

NOTES:

PART

The Techniques

Queen Nefertiti, c. 1360 BC

CHAPTER

Some Design Basics

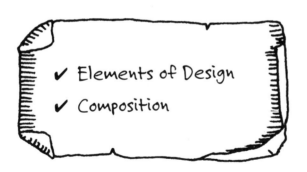

- ✔ Elements of Design
- ✔ Composition

In the long run it is easier to have a plan for a project than it is to wing it. Give some thought to what you are going to do before you do it. Try to make all your important design and color decisions <u>before</u> you start a project. Once a project is begun on an unstable or poorly built foundation, no matter how much time and effort are put forth, the result will probably suffer. Don't let the creative process become riddled with anxiety and uncomfortable decision making. When stuck or in doubt, try returning to the basics.

ELEMENTS OF DESIGN

Many art students identify themselves by their majors. They are graphic designers or animators or painters. But what if they change their major? What if later in their career they change studio concentration? I prefer to think of all students as artists or art students first, major second. One of the joys of art is the choice of different concentrations or focuses. Who says you have to choose one and that it is forever? No one. By thinking of yourself as an artist first, you are keeping yourself open to the opportunity to change if you want.

No matter what you major in, as an art student, especially a first-year art student, you will be making marks. Marks on paper, marks on computers, marks on fabric, even marks in clay. Marks can be simple; marks can be complex. They can be minimal like a dot; they can be big masses of solid shapes. Whatever they are, they make up the elements of design, and knowing how to use and place those marks efficiently and effectively will help you produce better projects.

The elements of design break down visual art into the most basic and common parts. You can use these principles how you wish. Like a composer who uses discordant combinations of notes to raise a reaction from the listener, the visual artist can do the same thing with elements of design. It is one thing when it is done with an intended purpose. But when done as the result of a poorly thought out or executed project, it sticks out like the proverbial sore thumb.

When taping a board or paper to a work surface, use a T-square or 90° triangle to line up the paper edge square to the drawing board or table edge. Later a ruler or triangle can be used accurately.

Give some thought to your choice and how you use these elements. Be able to defend your decisions. Learning how they work together is key. You will probably have a course dedicated entirely to the design basics. Some schools put all students from all art majors together in the same classes. Everyone learns the same thing when it comes to design. Some schools have design classes geared toward specific majors. A photo student, a sculpture student, a game designer, and a fashion student will all use the same information but they may be using it differently. The type of fabric, the subject, the feel of a surface, even the choice of what pencil to use can be affected by what design element you plan on using or emphasizing.

The Point

The point or the dot is the smallest of the visual
elements. Think of it as a small circular point in space. It
is the starting point of a line. A shape, a line, or even a
picture can be made up of points or dots. Pointillism is the
type or style of art, drawing, or painting that employs dots
or points to create the edges, shades, and textures of a
composition. Some impressionistic painters experimented
with this approach when applying marks to a paper or
canvas. Points or dots can be used to apply shadings
or tone to areas of a drawing or painting. They can
be added to the surface of a three-dimensional work to
add texture.

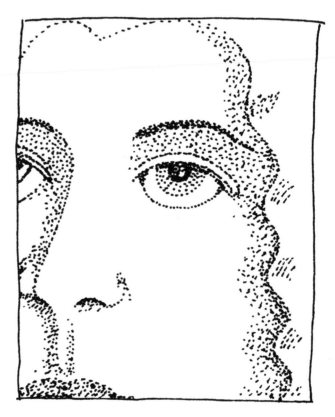

104

The Line

The line is a series of points lined up in succession so close that they cannot be distinguished from one another. Many lines placed together can indicate shading or texture. The shortest distance between two points is a straight line, but lines do not have to be straight, they can be curved or even squiggly. Lines can vary in thickness and length. A line can be a very versatile element to work with. Drawing lines with crayons is one of the first visual art techniques children learn.

Lines can also be used to indicate volume or shading in a drawing. Lines used in this manner are often referred to as <u>hatch lines</u> or <u>hatching</u>.

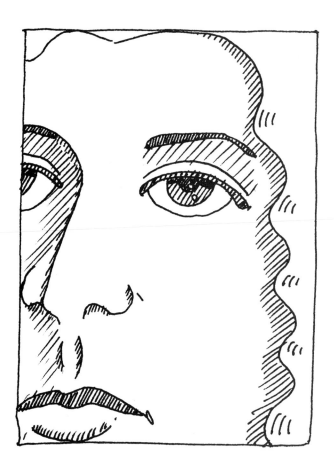

When a second series of lines is overlapped with the first
set of lines, the result is even more dramatic and is
referred to as <u>cross-hatching</u>. Cross-hatching is a way to
add depth and darkness without going to a solid black.
This method has been utilized in drawing and painting
alike for centuries.

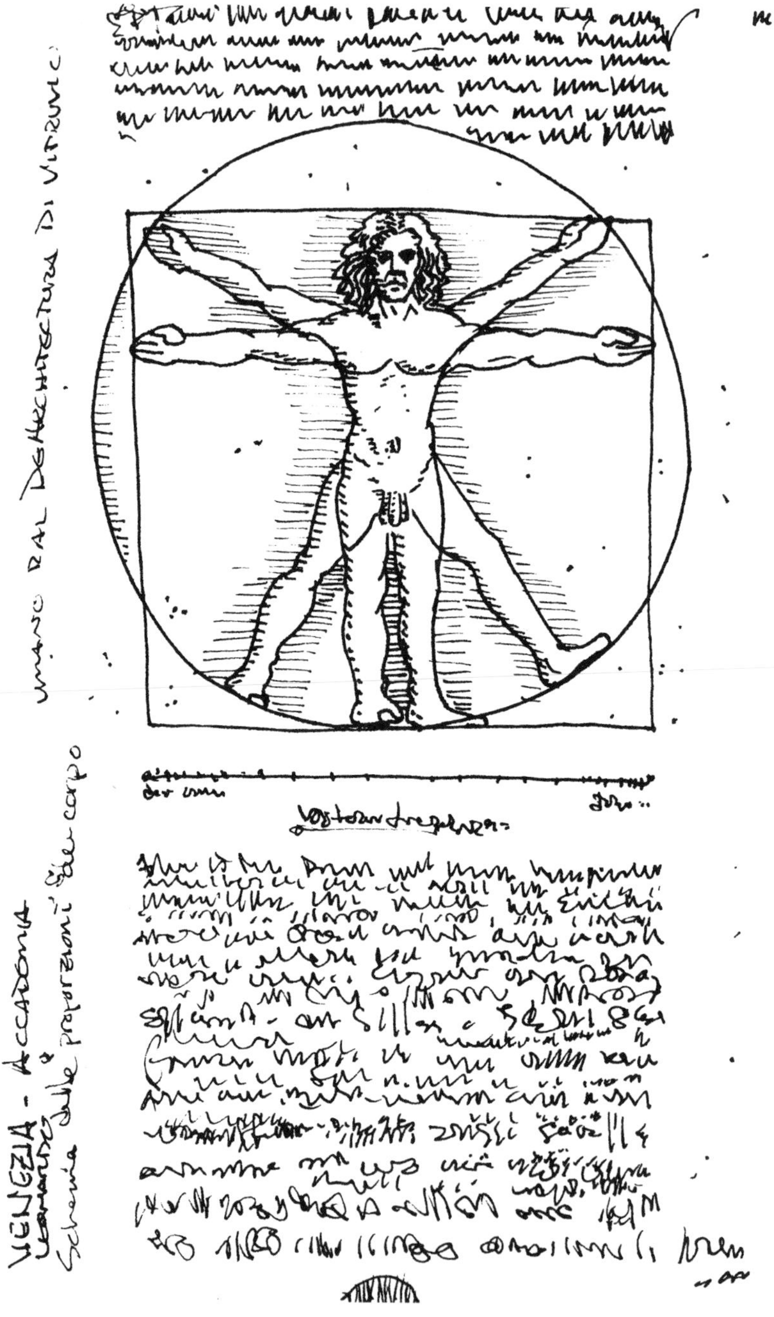
VENEZIA - ACCADEMIA
Leonardo
Schema delle proporzioni del corpo
umano dal De Architectura di Vitruvio

Look at the drawings and sketchbooks of Michelangelo or Leonardo da Vinci. Both of these artists employed the hatching technique to indicate volume and establish edges with weight, as did many artists throughout the centuries. The contemporary artist Robert Crumb, is a modern day master of this technique.

Shape

A shape is an enclosed area formed by a line connecting its starting point to its ending point. Shapes can be organic or geometric. Simple shapes that are created having no hard angles would be organic shapes, like the outline of a peanut or a kidney bean. Three points connected by means of three straight lines form the shape known as a triangle, a geometric shape. A circle and a square are other examples of geometric shapes.

109

Some shapes are simple, such as a circle or a rectangle. Some shapes are complex, made up from combinations of simple shapes. Shapes can have two or three dimensions. The concept of a shape can be a literal visual image such as a red rectangle painted on a canvas. Shape can be an imagined area in shape, or the boundaries of a paragraph of 12-point type printed on a page.

Color

Color is so complex, so deep an area, that there are entire courses devoted to nothing else. It is the reflective quality of an object and how our eyes and brains interpret those light waves reflected off of it. Light color objects reflect the light more than dark color objects, which absorb the light. But it is more than that. Color has the power to suggest temperature or atmosphere, even to affect a viewer emotionally.

The primary colors are red, yellow, and blue. They cannot be mixed from other colors, but they can be mixed to produce the secondary colors, orange, green, and purple. The primaries yellow and red make the secondary orange. The primaries yellow and blue make the secondary green. The primaries red and blue make the secondary purple.

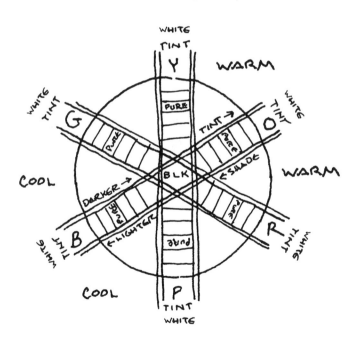

Adding white or light to a color creates a lighter tint of that color. Adding black or dark to a color creates a darker shade of that color. Based on this, there are countless possibilities on the variations of colors that can be produced.

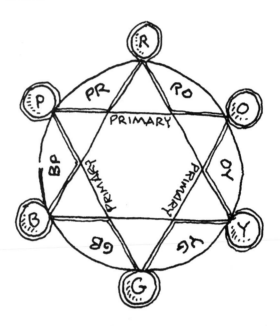

There are warm colors—yellow, orange, and red—and there are cool colors—green, blue, and purple.

Look at the colors as they are positioned on the simple color wheel in the accompanying illustration. Colors across from each other such as red and green or orange and blue are complimentary colors. That means that they generally work well together. They compliment each other. Further refining will show that orange/red generally compliments blue/green. Again, countless variations are possible. To go on further at this point is not necessary, as you will more than likely be studying color in depth.

Pattern

Patterns are a combination of lines, shapes, or colors that reoccur in a repetitive manner. Stripes are a pattern. Checks are a pattern. Patterns occur often in weaving. Paisley, houndstooth, and plaids are all patterns.

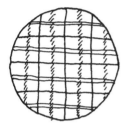 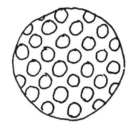 

Patterns are often used as decorative elements in fabrics, tile work, architecture, paintings, and graphic design. Patterns are all around us. Patterns are not as common in nature, but the industrial revolution has created tools that have allowed patterns to be taken to new heights. Look for them, create them, and try different combinations. Patterns can add detail and visual stimulation to an image or object. Patterns can also result in cluttered confusion.

Areas of patterns can be a nice contrast to large areas of plain or empty space. They provide a sort of balance. If the eye moves quickly across a large expanse of color, when it reaches the pattern, it stops for a moment, adjusting, resting, and even getting caught up and lost in the repetition of the pattern. Patterns can add just the right touch to a work of art. This does not mean that it is always appropriate to use patterns, but it is something that should not be overlooked as an option.

Texture

Texture can be thought of as the surface of an object. It can be tactile (something that can be physically felt), visual (something that can be seen), or both. Texture can have pattern and color. It can be smooth, rough, silky, wet, or prickly. How it is used depends on what medium is being used.

Texture can be the feel of a cat's fur, a burlap bag, a silk scarf, or a piece of sandpaper. Each of these has a specific feel or hand; each has a specific look. The addition of the visual of a texture in a work of art will suggest to the viewer the feel of that object. If it is an interactive work, the viewer may even be invited to feel the texture.

When finishing work on a drawing or painting, one of the last things to check is that the darkest darks and lightest lights are present.

COMPOSITION

The way the elements of design are laid out or used in a work of art to direct the viewer's eye make up the composition of the piece. Whether it's a page layout or a painting, composition is another one of those tools that the artist can use to create comfort or anxiety. Again that all depends on what the artist's intention is. Things to look for when analyzing a composition might include the following:

✔ Is the subject matter or theme unimpeded and free from distraction?

✔ Is the viewer's eye drawn or led to the most important part of the work first?

✔ Is it then directed on to the secondary components?

✔ Does the work feel stable or unstable?

✔ Does the balance and stability of the piece work with the theme of the piece?

Which of the layouts in the accompanying illustration is more stable? Both have the same rectangle and triangle. The inverted triangle almost feels like it wants to fall over. That might not be the best layout

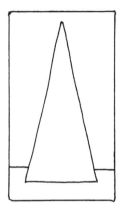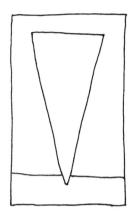

for an investment firm's annual report cover. But it might work if you wanted to suggest danger or tension. Stability and instability both have a place in composition and design.

Symmetry is a mirror effect in which the components are the same on both sides of the center. The human body and face are somewhat symmetrical. Two eyes, two ears, two arms, two legs, all in about the same position on each side of the center of the body. A composition in which the left side is an opposite duplicate of the right side, or mirror image, is a symmetrical composition.

Understanding these basic elements and how they can be used alone or with the others will give you the tools to direct viewers' eyes, to capture their attention, and to stimulate their minds and emotions. Artwork can be a very powerful tool when it comes to influencing people. And as always, remember that it should be used for good and not evil!

NOTES:

Theodora, The Court of Theodora, Mosaic, San Vitale c. 537

CHAPTER

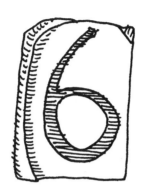

Drawing the Human Figure

✔ Who Needs It?
✔ About Models
✔ Is It Right?
✔ The Gesture
✔ The Robot
✔ Body Parts

At some point or another during your time at school, the human figure will probably find its way into your studies. Whether it is the focus of your work or just one course in your major, please take it seriously. How well you draw and represent the human figure may be used as a barometer of how well you can draw or represent anything else. After all, you are a human and unless you were raised by wolves, you have known the human form all of your life and you always have yourself for reference. You don't have to be a figurative artist or work with the most beautiful models to appreciate the human form. Understanding the figure and how it works makes it that much easier to draw, sculpt, or paint it. Even if you don't have a model, a mirror will do fine. Understanding the figure will prove to be a valuable tool in the studio.

Who Needs It?

Some may wonder why a graphic designer, multimedia artist, or industrial designer needs to know how to draw the human figure. You may even be asking yourself that very question, "Why do I have to study the figure?" Well, to draw it is to understand how it works. Knowing basic movements and proportions of the figure can make the difference in all sorts of projects.

When an industrial designer is designing a product for human use or interaction, knowledge of the human figure is essential. Imagine a chair designed by someone who did not understand the proportions of the human figure. How tall would the legs be? Would your feet be able to touch the floor when you sat on it? An art historian describing a figurative painting or sculpture will be able to express a greater understanding of a piece by having a working knowledge of the figure as a point of reference. A graphic designer working on a layout that includes a photograph of a person may give a comp or mock-up to a photographer from which to work. Movement, direction, mood, and expression all can be conveyed with a few simple lines. Understanding where and how to place those lines can make a difference in how an idea is presented and received.

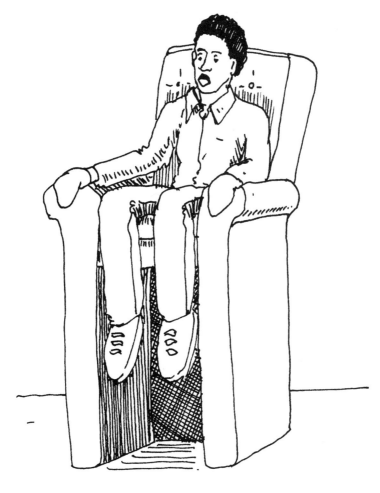

The human figure is foundation-level subject matter, a core skill in many programs of study. Some of you will continue to study it throughout your time at school, some will have but one class, some may even have none. This chapter is not meant to compete with or replace a course but rather to stress its importance and why it should not be taken lightly. Go to the library or bookstore and look at the figure drawing and anatomy books available. Even by casually flipping through the pages, you will start to absorb what you see. Exposing yourself to different philosophies and points of view on any subject will give you more ways of looking at things. How far you take it is up to you.

Studying the figure is kind of like math. Many art students question why they need math, yet many use it more often than they realize. The animator working at 30 frames or drawings per second uses math to estimate how many drawings will be needed to complete a certain timed sequence, an interior designer uses math to measure square footage, the potter uses it to measure and mix glazes. Just like math, studying the human figure may seem unnecessary to some, but it will come in handy at one time or another. You may not even realize that you are using it.

About Models

Throughout my education and life as an artist I have worked with many models. Some were beautiful human specimens, some were not. Beauty does not necessarily make for a good model. A perfect body does not necessarily make for a good model. It all depends on what your need is.

123

PERFECT FOR WHAT?

I once took an anatomy class where we used a number of different models—one week a man, one week a woman, all different ages, all different races, all different body types. At the same time we were looking at a skeleton for comparison of movement and proportion. In some cases it was easier to see the landmarks of the skeleton on the thinner models than on the heavier ones, but for the most part, they were all sufficient. The day we moved on to the muscles of the body, we had a new model, James. He might have been a gymnast, perhaps a body builder, maybe just a guy in great shape. Whoever he was, his muscle definition was so pronounced that seeing the origins and destinations of his muscles was easy. He was perfect for studying muscles. But his body lacked movement. It was tight, and even when relaxed he still looked the same as he did when holding a pose. My drawings of the heavy out-of-shape models were much more interesting to the eye, but for learning the muscles, James was perfect.

Sometimes it is the heavy model that makes for a more interesting drawing. The perfect figure for a print fashion ad, and the perfect figure depicting a librarian or a mom are not always the same. The fashion model is not the norm in our lives. True, there might be librarians and moms who look like they could be fashion models, but they are more the exception than the rule.

Some artists prefer to work with female models simply because the female body offers more curves and can be more interesting to draw. Even standing upright at attention, the female figure usually has more movement than the male figure. Don't be turned off by overweight or underweight models. Remember that this study is not about sexual attraction, it is about art. Keep the two apart. Even as a student, there is a professional decorum to abide by. Do not try to flirt with your model or make rude or suggestive comments. Keep it professional.

Be respectful of your models, for without them you would have to draw yourself, nude, staring into a mirror. And maybe, just maybe, you will need to do that some day. Models help us to create believable figures in our artwork.

Is It Right?

Everybody is different yet everybody is the same. Clothes are made in a range of sizes that cover most body types. Perhaps a little tailoring is needed, but the human species maintains pretty consistent physical characteristics. The proportions of the figure are somewhat the same for everyone. As a result, some different techniques have been developed to aid in establishing and checking a figure drawing. Two of the more widely used methods are looking for physical landmarks and counting heads. Neither is perfect all the time but may be close enough to keep your drawing in the right direction. Use these methods to help approximate and check your work. Eventually you will use the methods that work best for you and your needs.

Landmarks

When the figure is standing straight at eye level with no foreshortening, you might look for landmarks or points of reference. There are many schools of thought on this and numerous rules of thumb that are thought to be consistent on most people. Here are just a few of the many approximations and landmarks:

- ✔ From the top of the head, the nipples are about one-quarter of the way down the body.
- ✔ From the top of the head, the genitals are about half of the way down the body.
- ✔ From the top of the head, the knees are about three-quarters of the way down the body.
- ✔ The femur (bone from hip socket to knee) is twice as long as the skull.
- ✔ Middle of the figure for a man is at the pubic bone.
- ✔ Middle of the figure for a woman is just above the pubic bone.
- ✔ There is an eye width between the eyes.

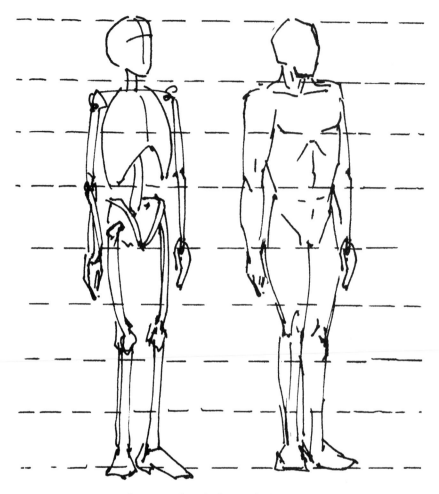

Landmarks of the male figure

Counting Heads

There are more than a few schools of thought on how many heads high the human body is. Some say the entire body is 7 heads tall, some say 7½, and others say 8.

128

Children are born with big heads and small bodies.
Young children are about 4 to 5 heads tall and grow into
their heads as they mature. Many of the elderly tend
shrink as their bones and muscles age.

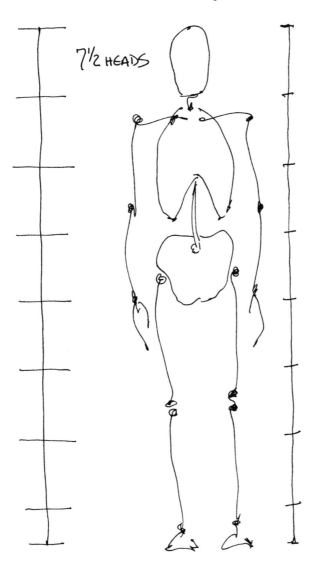

7½ HEADS

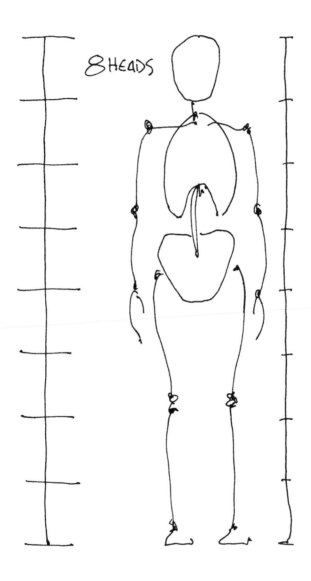

8 HEADS

Measuring

Start with his or her head. Holding your pencil in your outstretched hand, line up the end of the pencil at the top of the model's head, and slide your thumb down until it lines up with the model's chin. Hold it there. The distance is approximately one head.

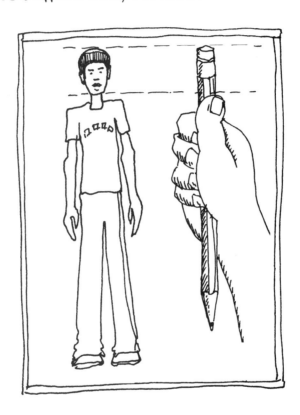

Now slide your hand down until the end of the pencil lines up with the bottom of the model's chin. Look where your thumb lines up on the model.

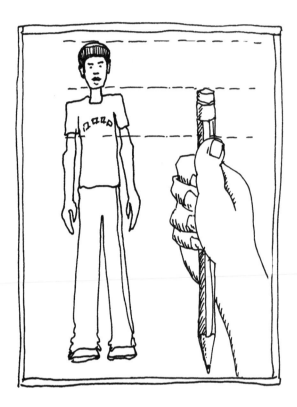

It is probably around the nipples or bottom of the sternum. Then take a visual reading on the sternum and move your hand down so the end of the pencil is on the sternum. Look at where your thumb is now.

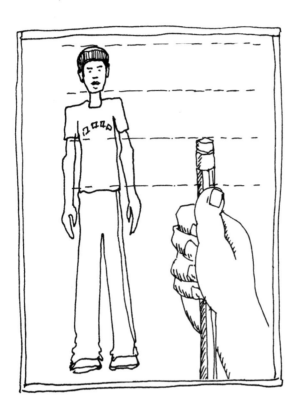

By repeating this process the length of the body, you can find visual reference points to ensure your drawing is properly proportioned. If your model is in a foreshortened view or not upright, the reference points will not apply to the proportions of the anatomy, but they will provide a way to compare your drawing against the model.

For Accuracy Sake

Consistency is key. When measuring with your pencil or brush, be sure that your arm's length from your eye is the same with each measurement you take. The distance you are from the model and sometimes the pose will determine how far you will extend your arm. Sometimes you will extend it fully; sometimes you will hold your elbow against your ribcage holding your pencil 12 inches from your nose. Either way is fine as long as you are consistent throughout the pose.

The Gesture

To draw the human figure well means finding the happy medium between capturing mass and movement. The ability to capture it using just a few lines drawn in a few minutes is key. Capturing the gesture and line of action sets the stage for a successful figure drawing. Some people look at the spine first. The gesture can follow the

spine to an extent, but the line of action also depicts
weight and the direction that the figure moves or flows.
The weight of the figure maybe planted firmly on one
end of the gesture-line. Then again the figure may be so
graceful that the gesture-line shows little weight at all.
Even a figure standing still may show some motion.

One way to practice finding the line of action on a figure
is to put tracing paper over pictures of people from
magazines. Look at the direction the mass of the figure
is taking. Now draw the one line that represents the
figure. There is usually a flow to it. Try this technique if
you are having problems finding the line of action and
capturing the gesture of the figure.

135

THE ROBOT

A figure is not a line; it is solid, it has weight and dimension. When the masses or parts of the body are simplified, the basic shapes can resemble a robot.

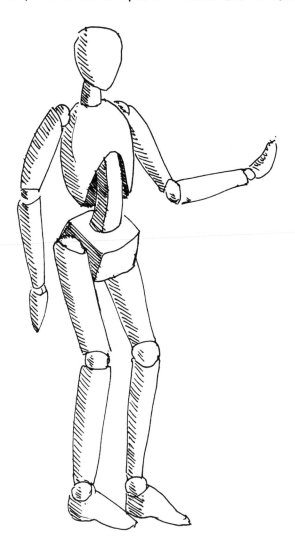

The spine is a long curved rectangle; the arms and legs are rectangles as well. The chest is an egg shape with an area in the lower front removed. The pelvic area is a box tilted forward. If you start with the gesture line and then add the shapes of the head, chest, and hips, the rest of the figure will follow if you remember the robot.

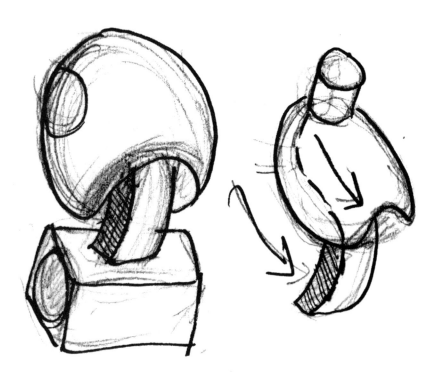

The figure looks kind of like the small wooden manikins sold in art supply stores. Keep that in mind next time you need a model and there are none to be found. With a mirror, a few simple measuring tips, and a wooden manikin, you'd be surprised how accurate your drawings can be.

137

138

BODY PARTS

Certain parts of the body can be problematic to draw, even intimidating. Hands and fingers, feet, and breasts are all body parts that can be troublesome to draw properly. Then there are the genitalia. For the student who has never drawn it before, it can be a difficult obstacle to overcome. If you are uncomfortable working from the model, let your instructor know. It is something you will have to get over if you plan on passing your Life Drawing or Anatomy classes. Remember there is nothing sexual about this. You are learning to draw the human form, and that means male and female forms alike. Be professional. A breast or penis is nothing more than another body part, just like an ear or elbow.

Hands and Feet

The human hand is a challenging subject to draw. Not only is it complex in its make up, but it can take on many different shapes and positions whether performing a task or at rest. There are a number of different approaches to drawing hands and fingers. One way is to break the hand down to a few basic shapes—the wrist joint, the body of the hand, the fingers, and the thumb. By simplifying to these basics, the challenge of blocking in a hand is lessened.

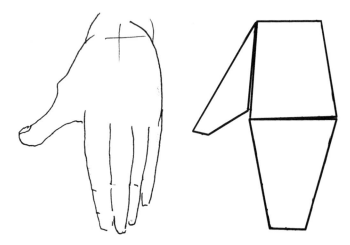

Try separating the first finger from the mass that makes up the fingers. Sometimes that is enough. Another way to capture the hand and fingers is to draw the shapes of the areas between the fingers. Look at the negative space; this technique changes the way the hand and fingers are thought of. You can avoid drawing hands and fingers only so long. This skill must be mastered.

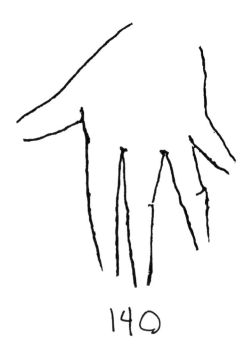

140

Many art students try to draw each finger individually, each joint, each crease in the skin. Sometimes it is simply too much information. Of course there will be exercises when the fingers and the proportions of each joint will be the assignment. In that case, refer to your anatomy book and your own hand. Be careful that the fingers don't end up looking like sausages.

Feet and Toes

Just like the hands and fingers, there are a number of different approaches to drawing feet and toes. One way is to break the feet down to a few basic shapes—the ankle joint, the body of the foot, and the toes.

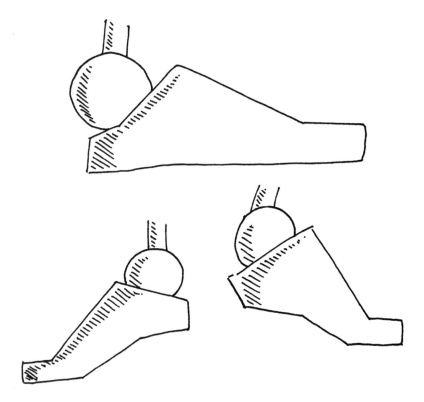

141

By simplifying to these basics, the challenge of blocking in a foot is lessened. Like the hand, the foot is made up of many bones and muscles. It is very complex, but not quite as versatile in its function as the hand. Toes are not as difficult as fingers because they are grouped tighter together and more often can be treated as a mass. When toes are drawn separately, they can be treated like fingers.

Look at how other artists have historically drawn the foot. Look at drawings, paintings, and even sculptures. I have found that seeing how something is treated in three dimensions has helped in my own approach to it in two dimensions.

Breasts, Male and Female

The makeup, design, function, and size of the breasts are gender specific. It is important to understand the anatomy involved. Since everyone's body is different, the following visual landmarks should be treated as flexible guidelines. The breasts lie on top of the chest muscles (pectoralis major) on each side of the sternum or center of the chest.

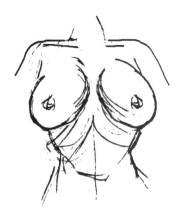

On the female, the breast is generally a half sphere, wider than high, with the widest part moving downward and away from the center of the chest. It is located somewhere between the third and sixth ribs. The nipple, a small darker protrusion, is often found below the center of the breast at about the level of the fifth rib. The nipple has a small ring around it known as the areola. It may also be darker than the rest of the breast. Nipples will all vary with weight and age, and don't necessarily have to do with the size of the breasts. Some younger developing or smaller breasts will be more conical in shape, and some older, larger breasts may lie flatter against the chest.

On the male, the breasts do not have the same function as the female's and as a result do not grow to the same size as the female counterpart. They are usually nothing more than nipples lying on top of a small area of fat, located just below the fourth rib. On men with more muscular chests, the nipples may appear to be closer together. On thinner or less muscular men, the nipples may appear to be farther apart. Heavyset men may have larger breasts, simply due to the fact that they are carrying more fat.

Drawing Faces

When drawing a person's face, look at the shadows cast in the eye socket areas, under the nose, lips, and chin. Sometimes cheekbones also cast shadows. If you have a hard time seeing them, you may need to adjust the light or even squint a little to put things out of focus.

The shapes of these shadows are created by the planes of the face, and while we all have the same planes, the size and shape of them vary enough to give each of us our own individual look. A likeness of someone can be found without line. Try adding line after the shadows are found. You may not need that many of them to get the level of detail that you desire.

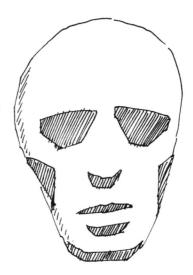

People come in all shapes and sizes. Their characters and attitudes may be evident in the way they carry

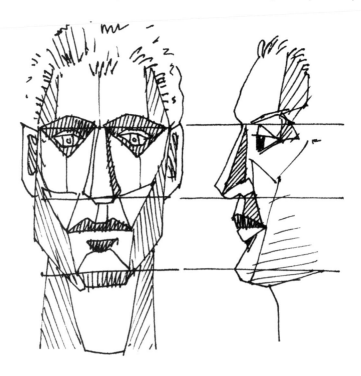

144

themselves. You can see it any day. Watching people is not a pastime unique to artists, but an artist can take it to another level by sketching what he sees. Next time you feel like watching people, get out your sketchbook and enjoy the free models that pass by you.

NOTES:

Jamb figures, Chartres Cathedral c. 1225

Creative Problem Solving

✔ Try Something Different

✔ Different Approaches

✔ Using Your Memory

✔ Art That Catches Attention

✔ Symbolism

Conceptual thinking requires the ability to think beyond the obvious. Symbolism, comparison, parallels, reflections, expectations, knowledge of culture and society, all of these things can play a role in conceptual problem solving. Here are a few ways to look at creative problems and few ways to solve them with imaginative solutions.

TRY SOMETHING DIFFERENT

Looking for a great idea? Got creative block? Try something different. A boring or dull subject can invite creative block. Difficult and overwhelming projects can make the mere thought of completing the project an unattainable goal, let alone finishing it with a strong creative solution. Sometimes it helps to think of the obvious; sometimes the obvious should be avoided. How do you know when to do what? There are a number of ways to approach a problem, and it is up to each artist to find what works best for him or her.

Visit the library or bookstore. There are books written specifically on this subject, not to mention magazine

A string or a shoelace will work as a compass for drawing larger circles. Tie a loop in each end of the string. Tack the string through one loop to the center of where you want the circle. Put your pencil through the other loop and while holding the tacked center in place, extend the string as far as it can go away from the center. Placing the point of the pencil on the paper, rotate around the center using the tacked end as your pivot point.

articles. Do a search in the library, not just on the Internet. Do a search in a toy store. Do the search with a goal, but do it with an open mind.

Be More Descriptive

It helps to have as much information about a subject as possible before you start a project. If there is no additional information, look for descriptive words and phrases that might give a better picture of the subject. Ask yourself (and maybe your teacher or client), Can I embellish the information I have? If so, how much?

It is said that a picture is worth a thousand words. But sometimes a few words can change the context of that picture. By simply adding an adjective to the name of the object or subject, a new vision can surface. Maybe this new vision will be more interesting or even exciting to work on.

Imagine a chicken. . . .

Now imagine a chunky
chicken.

You have a different
image by simply adding
an adjective. Now add
another adjective...
imagine a striped
chunky chicken.

150

Yet another image. By further describing the subject, the artist has more information to work from. It is good to have adjectives handy. Keep a list in your sketchbook. The following list is one to start with—use one, use several.

New	Spaced-out	Hairy	Impatient
Old	Wavy	Slim	Sexy
Worn	Striped	Husky	Drab
Shiny	Dotted	Tall	Exotic
Stretched	Textured	Short	Angry
Dented	Rough	Fat	Dark
Rusted	Smooth	Thin	Moody
Spanking	Slippery	Bald	Mean
Improved	Moving	Toothless	Important
Mature	Classy	Cultured	Innocent
Young	Stylish	Single	Thankful
Studious	Important	Married	Anxious
Broken	Winning	Lying	Late
Wrapped	Spinning	Gross	Early
Quiet	Agreeable	Loud	Gourmet
Reserved	Flaming	Hungry	Packed
Daring	Burning	Starved	Perfect
Dirty	Signing	Stuffed	Flawed
Soiled	Flowered	Crazy	Loud
Cracked	Perfumed	Lost	Dark
Howling	Delicate	Content	Fake
Weathered	Screaming	Illegal	Hot
Firm	Fighting	Righteous	Empty
Flabby	Super	Beautiful	Average
Tired	Thankful	Smart	Simple
Musical	Gracious	Dumb	Plaid
Bilingual	Warmhearted	Happy	Lucky
Big	Coldhearted	Sad	Cranky
Little	Hurried	Wild	Sick
Stern	Chunky	Mild	Greedy
Mediocre	Angular	Hurt	

151

Work under Different Conditions

Try working at different times of day. Some people are better at writing in the morning and doing artwork in the afternoon or evening. Some people are early birds, some are night owls. Some are both.

I write best first thing in the morning. I can roll out of bed, grab a cup of coffee, and start writing. I am better in the studio in the afternoon and evening. But what happens if I roll out of bed at 6:30 a.m. and start working in the studio? Or what about setting the alarm clock for 3:30 a.m. and getting up to work on a project? The result could be surprising. Find out how you work best and not so best. Use it to your advantage. Get to know yourself and how you work and learn.

Look at both craft and concept. Craft is the quality and skill put into the execution of the media for the project. Concept is the idea and how it is presented. High-quality precision and detailed work is usually achieved when the artist is totally awake and conscious. But ideas, ideas can come in dreams or when half asleep.

If time affords it, try staying awake for 24 or 36 hours before the brainstorming for an idea begins. Lack of sleep can cause the brain to work in different ways. Always be safe and never put yourself in harm's way when doing this. Try this at home, maybe when others are around. Be in a position that a bed or couch is nearby.

Keep a pad or sketchbook near your bed. If you come up with an idea while sleeping, jot it down as soon as you wake up. Being sick is a miserable thing, but a fever can produce altered thoughts and even hallucinations. If at all possible, try to remember the ideas and thoughts that run through your head when running a fever.

Try Many Options/Answer the Problem Assigned

Some projects will be simple exercises, some will be comps, and some will be multiple complex exercises combined into larger productions. A beautifully rendered or executed mediocre idea will present one way; a simply drawn great idea will present another way. Is a beautifully rendered great idea the best of both? Sometimes yes, sometimes no.

An artist should always strive for quality. Work to astonish people. Strive for magnificent solutions. Always look at the project criteria before starting. Be sure to answer the problem assigned. It is easy to be drawn into an interpretation that is not really what the instructor is asking for. Make sure the answer is appropriate before starting the final project.

DIFFERENT APPROACHES

While in graduate school I took a conceptual illustration course with an instructor by the name of Lou Carbone. Lou shared with the class some different ways to look at a project, and he used a few illustrators and their approaches as examples. The following approaches are my notes from the class directly from my sketchbook. I've translated the shorthand. This is what I got out of Lou's presentation and what I recall of it.

The Spontaneous Approach

Get all of the information that you know about the project, all the details and criteria that must be included or represented. Get focused, concentrate on the problem. In one minute, do as many quick thumbnail sketches as possible.

Then start editing and refining from there. This is a way to get right into a solution. It forces quick thinking. The downfall may be the great ideas that got away.

The More Deliberate Approach

Get ready to do 50 thumbnails. Define your requirements, any restrictions, limits, rules, or information that must be observed. Define the purpose of the project. Then create as many thumbnails as possible quickly and spontaneously, without censoring or rationalizing. Let go, explore the unknown. Not just the beautiful, but the ugly as well. Learn to relax your mind. Allow for the unique ideas that at first seem inappropriate.

Now based on the thumbnails, take one or more of the best thumbnails and using good reference material, create a thumbnail for each of the following scenarios or versions: dumbest, most monumental, most mediocre, most passionate, weirdest, sexiest, most disgusting, most fantastic (imaginative), most descriptive, funniest, artistic, and most commercial. This exercise should take less than an hour. Spend five minutes on each thumbnail.

Now based on those 12 concepts, get specific. Do a few 10-minute thumbnails. The best commercial solution, the most artistic, and the one you, the artist, wants to do most. Then get some input from your (art director), instructor, or a fellow student whose work you respect. Decide, refine, and finish the project. An hour or two is a small amount of time to spend on a well-thought-out solution. It is always better to start with a strong idea.

USING YOUR MEMORY

Sometimes the memory of something is stronger than any make believe or manufactured version. Tap into your memories. Remember the worst thunderstorm or bad weather you've been in. What about the playground at your elementary school, do you remember that? What about other things? Can you remember what the dashboard of your car looks like? Or the front of your house? Try to make a concerted effort at remembering what you are looking at. Use your eyes and your mind as a camera. Look at something. Now close your eyes . . . do you see that object on the back of your eyelids? If not look again, then close your eyes . . . see it now? When you do, let your eyes and your mind be a camera shutter and click the image into your memory. Look to See to Remember!

A Great Art Educator

Look to See to Remember! Every Saturday morning for four years Mr. Fitzpatrick stressed the importance of observation. Look to See to Remember! He stressed the importance of memory.

Joseph C. Fitzpatrick taught the Tam O' Shanter Saturday art classes at the Carnegie Museum for many decades. I studied with him in the midsixties and can still remember him on the stage. He influenced thousands of Pittsburgh's gifted young artists. I was one of the fortunate ones, and he influenced me at a young age as well. I knew I would be an artist. At an older age I knew I would be an art teacher. Mr. Fitzpatrick gave me a head start on the field.

Art That Catches Attention

It is very cool to create a work of art that causes viewers to do a double take. But how do you do that? By creating a well done piece with a great idea. If not a great idea, one that causes people to stop and think. What makes people stop and think? Things that are impossible, or fantastic, or things that don't happen every day. Once in a lifetime things. To catch attention is to take control of the viewer, even if it is just for a few seconds.

What If?

The "what if?" scenario is a good way to get a viewer's attention. By taking the normal or expected situation or action and offering a fantastic or impossible twist to it, the artist can create a project that captures the viewer off guard. This is the perfect way to dazzle the viewer.

What if pigs could fly? How would this be depicted? What about elephants? Dumbo? What if the earth were square? Maybe this should be a 3D piece. Talk about symbolism. What if the good did die young? Who might they be? Where would we be? What if brown cows gave chocolate milk? What if a "what if" came true? Putting a man on the moon. Who would have thought?

Possible But Not Probable Situations

Ever try a tuna milkshake? Yuk! Not likely, but it is possible, just not probable. I grew up eating banana and mayonnaise sandwiches; they are actually quite tasty. Tuna milkshakes are not. What made the movie "Rocky" so successful? It was possible, just not probable.

Looking out of the second floor window of a downtown office building and seeing a boat mast? It's possible if the boat is being towed on a trailer through town, but it's just not probable. The sight would still attract attention. What about a typical 70-year-old grandmother playing pool with a bunch of bikers in a bar? What about a movie star being elected governor of California? It is possible, just not probable. What about it happening twice? These are memorable events and situations. Do not forget the possible but not probable situation.

SYMBOLISM

Symbolism in art can be thought of as a visual image that can give another or multiple meanings to an idea. What about a shadow? A cast shadow indicating a different action than what the subject casting it is really doing can give a second meaning to a picture. A reflection that is not true to its subject works the same way. Using black and white in a portion of a color work or vice versa can indicate a dream or different time. During the renaissance, symbolism was used often in religious art. A dog might signify loyalty, for example.

Subliminal messages can be placed in your art. A subliminal message is a message that is hidden or very, very subtle. In a video or film that runs at 30 or 24 frames per second, a single frame with a different image might be embedded in the midst of a sequence. It might not be visible, but the mind catches it. So powerful is the effect that the use of subliminal messages can be looked at as unethical. Don't put things in your work that you will regret later. As stated before, art is a powerful tool and should be created and used responsibly.

WRONG NUMBER

I've been told a story about an editorial cartoonist for a large metropolitan newspaper who, after a messy divorce, placed his ex-wife's telephone number in one of his cartoons. Of course the ex got phone calls and the reason why was easily traced back to the artist. The way I hear it, he was promptly fired.

However you decide to handle a project, strive for that great solution. Create a work that not only is well crafted but well thought out, too. Strive to astonish. I think of it as the Whoa Factor. Try to create work that causes viewers to say "Whoa" when they view it.

NOTES:

163

PART

The Tools

Mona Lisa, Leonardo da Vinci, 1506

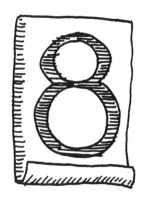

Tools of the Trade

- ✔ Artists' Tools and Supplies
- ✔ Caring for Materials and Tools
- ✔ Traditional Art Tools
- ✔ Digital Art Tools
- ✔ Finding the Tools

Many kindergarten through 12th grade (K-12) art educators are taught to teach art through any number of media and tools. Their studies are often a mixture of education courses teamed with studio courses. The studio coursework may be diverse to include many different studio areas, making for well-rounded teachers. Someone who can teach drawing, painting, ceramics, printmaking, computer graphics, jewelry, and sculpture can provide a good overall view of the visual arts. Generally that is the idea. But like any other artist, there is often one area that they prefer or in which they excel. Often that area is given more time in the classroom. Is that wrong?

Which is better? To have an instructor who teaches one or two things well and is enthusiastic about them, or to have an instructor who covers everything but in a less-than-enthusiastic manner? As a result, some students enter art school or college having strong experience in one area while being totally ignorant about everything else. Others enter college with a broad background but little focus or experience in what they want to major in. Knowing the different supplies and tools for a studio area or medium is essential to the successful execution of projects in that chosen area.

ARTISTS' TOOLS AND SUPPLIES

With students coming from so many different backgrounds, having studied or not studied with so many different teachers, it's hard to get an idea of what people know when it comes to materials and supplies. Some students have experienced much, enjoying great facilities at a school with a healthy budget for the arts. But if your previous art experiences were from an inner city school or a school in a rural area with little or no budget for art supplies, you may know little more than pencils, crayons, and manila paper. This is not to belittle the importance of pencils and crayons, for beautiful and moving works of art can be created with them, but many options are available for you to choose from when it comes to art supplies and tools.

You will learn what to use and why to use it. Take care of your tools and supplies and they will last. Buy the best

tools and supplies that you can afford, because it usually makes a difference. It's OK to start with student-grade materials in the beginning (with your instructor's approval), but don't be afraid to upgrade if you will be using the materials on a regular basis.

What you ultimately use for the tools of your trade will depend heavily on your major. Scissors and a sewing machine are more important to a fashion design student than to a video student. The computer animator will have a greater need for an external storage drive than a ceramics major will. The point is, the tools and supplies that you use in your major will probably be major specific. What you use in your first year or foundation courses will be more general and overlap across all majors. Certain tools are common to all artists at one time or another. This chapter gives a general overview of some of the tools used in foundation-level courses.

CARING FOR MATERIALS AND TOOLS

Artists' tools and materials can be expensive, very expensive. Luckily they come in a number of grades. There are generally a student grade, an intermediate grade, and then a professional grade. Each of these divisions may have a subdivision as well, but at least the option is there to start small and work up as warranted. As you find your focus, you can upgrade the tools as you go. By starting with an economical grade, you will tend to appreciate the better quality products as you move up to them. If you start with the best, you may not appreciate what you have. A simple mistake or misuse will be less painful (and expensive) if you have to replace a student-grade item instead of a professional-grade item.

Have you ever left a brush sitting in a glass of water only to find that later when you remove it, the brush hair is bent and curves to the side? Or have you ever left a jar of rubber cement open only to return to a jar of rubber? Materials are expensive and it is important to get into the practice of taking care of them. Have a place to keep them. Budget yourself some time for cleanup at the end of every work session.

When using paints or pastes with screw-off lids, try to wipe clean the threading of the jar or bottle before replacing the lid. Keep a rubber kitchen jar opener with your paint supplies.

Use your tools and materials for what they were intended. One of the quickest ways to ruin a tool is to use it for the wrong type of task. A good example is to use your watercolor brush only with watercolors. Even though acrylics are water based, they tend to affect the hair of the brush. Brushes don't seem to absorb water the same after being used with acrylics, and there is usually some residue of dried acrylics in the hair near the ferrule (the metal band that attaches the hair to the handle) when you are finished. Don't even think about using a watercolor brush with oil paint. It will never be the same again, at least for use with watercolors. Scissors are for cutting, not to be used as pliers.

There is a proper tool for each job. Use it. If you do not have it, get it. If you cannot afford it or find it, see if you can borrow it. Just be sure to respect it and return it in the condition that you got it. Many people will not lend tools for the very good reason that they may have loaned a tool and gotten it back in poor condition or maybe never at all. If you loan out your tools, keep track of who has them. The same goes for your books.

Health and Hazards

For years artists worked with materials that were hazardous to their health. I guess it was the price of doing art. Not anymore. Certain materials have been banned; others have been taken off of the shelves of art stores. In the past 25 years there has been an organized effort to label materials that could be harmful to you. Precautions should be taken. Solvents are to be treated with respect, both in use and disposal. Use care when handling and disposing of residue and waste products from the creation of your art. Read the labels on the materials that you use; they are there for a reason. Heed the warnings. Be sure to observe the precautions in the following list:

- ✔ Wear respirators when appropriate.
- ✔ Keep away from flame when instructed.
- ✔ Use hazardous materials in a well-ventilated area.
- ✔ Protect your eyes and ears when appropriate.
- ✔ Keep materials out of direct sunlight, if directed.
- ✔ Wash hands thoroughly after using.
- ✔ Rest eyes when working with computers and video.

When you start school will you be bringing supplies with you, or will you start fresh and build your studio from scratch? Be careful when packing and moving materials. Pay special attention to items that are flammable, heavy, fragile, or can spill.

Some schools put together a studio package or kit of tools for every student to begin with. It might be digital, it might be traditional, it might be both. This kit helps eliminate confusion and guarantees that everyone will be working with the same set of tools. Whether a piece of computer software or a specific type of glue, use the tools and supplies suggested by your instructors and appropriate for the project at hand.

TRADITIONAL ART TOOLS

Traditional tools have changed little in the past few years, but there are always innovations and somebody trying to invent the better mousetrap. Feel free to experiment with the new products on the market. Ask yourself, Does the new product have the same properties of the original product that it was derived from? Is it better? Is it better for your needs?

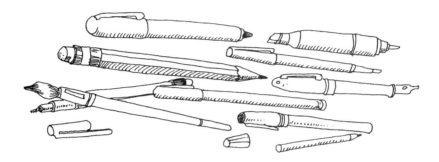

There are so many different tools and media to choose from it is hard to decide what to include and where to start. This list only covers some of the basics. You are encouraged to add to it as you see fit. The comparing and sharing of your findings with friends and classmates enlightens everyone involved.

Drawing

One of the earliest experiences we have with art is in the form of drawing. It can be done with any number of materials from crayons on the wall to sticks in the dirt to fingers on foggy car windows. This early form of expression lets us know that we can take ideas and images in our heads and transform them into visual images for others to see. Some artists choose drawing as their primary focus in the studio. For others it is merely a step toward more complex endeavors.

PENCILS

Pencils come in different shapes and sizes and with different cores to them, each having something different to offer. In time past, some pencils had lead inside them. It was soft and left a line when rubbed against paper. Paints also had lead in them, but it was discovered that the lead was not healthy for the user. So lead was banished from the pencil and most paint. Today replacement refills and points for mechanical pencils are still referred to as leads even though they are not made of it. For black and shades of gray, graphite is now the choice of pencil manufacturers and users. The graphite pencil comes in a full range of densities, from 9H to 9B with 9H being the hardest/lightest and 9B being the softest/darkest. The standard school pencil is usually a 2 or HB, which falls in the middle of the road as far as graphite pencils go. The harder the graphite (larger number on the H side, lower number on the B side), the lighter the line will be. It will stay sharp longer and smudge less. The softer the graphite (smaller number on the H side, higher number on the B side), the darker the line will be and easier to smudge. It will require sharpening more frequently and can be messier if used carelessly.

Charcoal pencils also come in a variety of densities usually ranging from HB to 6B, again with the higher number designating the softer and darker pencil. Some brands may label these as light, medium, and dark. These are great for drawing as well as detail when working with vine charcoal. Sometimes a white pencil accompanies sets of charcoal pencils. Some charcoal pencils are made with paper wrapped around them and a string to pull that

Do not drop your pencils! If you do, the graphite or pigment stick inside may crack or break in many different places. Then each time you sharpen the pencil the point will slip out of the wooden casing and you will have to sharpen it again. This continues until there is no pencil left. In many cases a dropped pencil is the same as a dead pencil. A dropped box of pencils will surely lead to more sharpening and more frustration.

exposes more charcoal as the user unravels the paper. Both charcoal pencils and graphite pencils are available individually and in sets.

Moving from black and white to color, the transition begins with Conté pencils. Similar to Conté crayons, these pencils have a chalky feel and can be smudged and blended on the paper. Conté pencils are available in sanguine (a brick red/brown), sepia (a darker warm brown), white, and a number of densities of black. Conté pencils should be sharpened with a razor blade or knife.

Color pencils are used for many different reasons and purposes and come in a variety of colors and types. There are pencils with a waxy feel. The colors are brilliant and the pencils can be sharpened to a point for detail work. When applied intensely, these can simulate paint. Some people blend them with clear blender markers, lighter fluid, or rubber cement thinner. Be cautious when using any solvent as some are flammable, some are toxic, and some are both. Then there are pastel pencils, which also come in many colors. They are chalkier in consistency, allowing the user to smudge and blend after applying them to paper. Watercolor pencils can be a good transitional medium when moving from drawing to painting. A wet brush run over a pencil-colored area on dry paper will yield a watercolor wash. The pencil drawn directly on wet or damp paper can yield a smooth line with a slight bleeding of the color. Any and all of these color pencils work well in mixed media. The waxy pencils work especially well with markers and they all work well with watercolors and gouache.

For working on china, glass, film, or acetate there is the china marker or chinagraph pencil, which is resistant to water, yet easily removable with a dry cloth. These are available in a limited number of colors and sometimes the only medium that will work.

Mechanical or drafting pencils have a body like a pen but draw like a pencil. They use graphite or colored lead refills that are available in a number of thickness and densities. The pencil bodies vary in shape and grip or texture. Cost is reasonable. These types of pencils have been around for years and have become somewhat collectable. Depending on make and model, they can run upward of a few hundred dollars. They were often sold as a set with a fountain pen, which is also a great drawing tool.

CHARCOAL

Charcoal is pretty much just what the name implies. It is the carbon by-product that is the result of burning wood. It smudges easily and has been a favorite drawing medium among artists for years. It is not for those who are afraid to get their hands dirty. For those people, there are charcoal holders available. Much like the

In a pinch, use aerosol hairspray if you have no fixative for your charcoal or pastel works. <u>Always</u> test on a scrap of the same paper with the same medium on it before you spray your project. Don't hold the can too close to the paper; allow at least 12 inches.

mechanical pencil that holds the graphite lead, charcoal holders are adjustable metal or plastic tools that hold a vine or stick charcoal so the hand doesn't touch the medium, just the holder.

Vine and willow charcoals are soft and produce smooth dark lines. A thin stick, this charcoal may have an occasional hard spot in it and can break easily if too much pressure is applied. The sticks are about 5 inches long and vary in thickness because they are a natural product. They range from thin (about 3–4 millimeters) to extra thick (10–15 millimeters), packaged by size or assortment. For larger projects there are larger-size charcoals available. Jumbo sticks or tree sticks are closer to 20 millimeters in diameter and blocks are about 2 x 5½ inches. These are good for blocking in murals, signs, and life-size drawings.

Compressed charcoal, which is more like a chalk or pastel in consistency, is a compressed powder that is available in different sizes and degrees of hardness. These sticks are generally available in soft, medium, and firm, with a white charcoal also offered. These charcoals are good for shading and blending and generally have no hard spots.

Just as charcoal and Conté are manufactured as pencils, graphite and Conté are also manufactured as sticks. These range in hardness from 4B (very soft) to HB (medium firm). The Conté is also available in white, sanguine, and sepia. Again, these are sold individually and in sets.

Both charcoal and graphite are available in powder forms. Powders can be messy if not handled carefully, but they can also produce beautiful shadings. Paper stubs and erasers are used for blending and subtracting areas. Powders also work well on frosted acetate and paper. Paper stubs and tortillons made of tightly spiral-wound paper with points on the end are used for blending and smudging charcoal and pastels. Because of the point, detailed areas can be smudged and blended easier than with your finger.

ERASERS

Sometimes I think that erasers are counterproductive. Draw a line, erase a line, draw a line, erase a line. Then there are the times that I thank the lucky stars that someone invented them. Erasers can be considered specialty items. Different ones work better on different surfaces and with different media. Some types of erasers can get old and stale. Have you ever been using a pencil, turned it over to use the eraser and it was a petrified piece of useless rubber? There are replacement erasers for pencil ends that come in your favorite cartoon character. They may be cute but will they work? Some will, some won't. Get erasers that work. Get rid of old ones that are hard and smear your work or worse yet, damage your paper surface.

There are erasers for different mediums—ink, charcoal, and pencil. Then there are erasers for different

179

surfaces and types of paper or vellum. There are even electric and air erasers. Dry cleaning pads, used for cleaning dirt and smudges off a paper, will not harm the drawing on it. There are also eraser templates or shields to mask and protect areas when erasing. A chamois skin can also be considered an eraser. It is a natural product that can be used for shading, blending, polishing, or just wiping charcoal off the paper. Chamois skin absorbs water and can be washed when it is too dirty. Try to have a variety of erasers in your supplies and use the proper ones for your chosen medium.

CRAYONS

When we think of crayons, we often think of the eight fat crayons we used in elementary school. Many of us eventually moved on to the 64-color set with the built-in sharpener in the back. That set is a great, economical way to have a full-color palette at your disposal.

There are cheap crayons and there are expensive ones. Usually you get what you pay for. When we think of crayons we think of a wax-based medium. Think back to some of those art projects from elementary school. Placing wax paper over top of a crayon drawing, then ironing it. Or laying down the undercoloring for a scratchboard. You probably already know the technique; now that you are a serious art student, maybe it's time to try those techniques again. There are also oil crayons and water-soluble crayons. Each type of crayon is a little different and should not be overlooked as a serious drawing medium. Crayon works by both Seurat and Klimt remind me of just how nice crayons can look.

PASTELS

Pastels are another popular color drawing media.
Soft pastels are a powdered pigment compressed and
held together by a natural (sometimes clay) binding
ingredient. Similar to crayon in that they are color sticks
usually sold in sets, they also give the ability to smudge
and blend like charcoal. Sort of like the rich man's color
chalk. Pastels can be dusty and crumble, although
modern pastels generate less dust than older sets. If you
come across an old set at a yard sale they are worth
investigating. A quality 40-piece set of pastels can run
well over a hundred dollars. For a full compliment of
colors, a quality two-hundred-piece set can run more than
four hundred dollars. These are serious drawing and
painting media and should be cared for appropriately.

There are also oil pastels, which are not as messy and do
not crumble as much as the powder pastels. They are
smooth, light, fast, clean, opaque, and brilliant. Some
painters will work these pastels into oil paintings as they
offer a feel and line that a brush cannot.

Visit an art store and look at the varieties available.
Many products are available that combine qualities of
each; hybrids so to speak. Ask if there are samples to try.
If one of your classmates has a type of pastel you are not
familiar with, ask to try one. It would be financially
prohibitive to have a set of each of the many products
available, but each is worth investigating.

PENS

One of the oldest of artists' tools, the pen continues to
evolve to this day. A stick, a feather, a piece of bamboo

cut on an angle—all pens. Usually used with ink (although dyes and paints also work), pens are often associated with writing, but as a drawing tool pens offer a quality of line no brush ever can. Some pens are dipped in ink every few minutes, lines, or words to refill the reservoir. Others can be filled, allowing the user to work uninterrupted for extended periods of time. Disposable pens can be used for days, even months, before exhausting the ink supply, and then they are simply thrown away.

Pens come with felt tips, ballpoints, razor tips, or brush tips. They can be inexpensive, costing a few cents or they can be pricey, costing hundreds of dollars. There are so many types of pens on the market it is hard to decide which to use. Just walk down the pen aisle of an office supply store and you will see what I mean. When you find one that you like, make note of the brand and model. Dip pens have changeable nibs or points that can offer a variety of different line widths. Slight pressure can also be applied to these pens, changing the thickness of the line. Technical pens have interchangeable tips, each with a specific line width. If pressure is applied to these tips, the point will probably break or bend. Ballpoint pens can be a wonderful choice when drawing with ink. The combination of ink type and point allow for middle tones and shading, as well as line. Pen and ink works well alone or with watercolor or ink washes. Be sure to use the appropriate ink and pen.

Ink comes in water soluble and waterproof. Be sure to use the proper inks for your projects and needs. When left in technical and fountain pens for extended periods waterproof inks can dry and clog the pen. The task of cleaning them is not easy and is sometimes frustrating to

182

the point of depositing the pen in the trash. When not using refillable pens for extended periods, empty and clean them, refilling them when needed.

MARKERS

Much like crayons, pastels, and color pencils, markers also come in a full assortment of colors. They can be bought individually or in sets and can run into hundreds of dollars. Fortunately they run out of ink one at a time, making it affordable to replace dried-out markers. Art directors and designers still use marker renderings for comps and layouts, so the different colors are labeled allowing for consistency.

Markers come with a variety of point sizes or interchangeable nibs. Some markers even have a broad chisel tip on one end and a fine point on the other. Markers work well with color pencils and some suppliers manufacture both, using the same color identification system. They are available in both warm and cool shades of gray in 10 percent increments and have clear blending markers as well. Markers can bleed when used on certain papers. As a result, bleed-proof marker paper is available. Sometimes color bleeding can be a desirable effect. Be careful where you draw with markers as they can bleed through a paper onto the surface below.

Paint

In your foundation classes you will probably have a design or color class that requires you to use paint. Paint is a solution of pigment (color) and a vehicle (liquid) to mix it with so it can be applied to different surfaces. The

184

viscosity or thickness of the liquid is determined by the ratio of pigment and vehicle in the mixture. Like any other medium, once you understand it, it is easier to make the proper choices.

Water- and alcohol-based paints dry quickly because the liquid they are mixed with evaporates more quickly. Oil-based paints take longer to dry. Additives are available to retard the drying of water-based paints or accelerate the drying of oil-based paints. Different types of paints vary in their degree of opacity. Being thick in viscosity does not always mean the paint will be opaque and cover what's under it. Some colors such as ultramarine blue are more transparent by nature.

When painting, instead of using pure black paint, try mixing burnt umber with ultramarine blue to create a different black.

Chances are you will be using water-based paints in your foundation classes. Clean up is easier, drying time is faster, and there are no fumes to deal with. Watercolor, gouache, tempera, and acrylics are probably the main four paints.

Gouache (pronounced as one syllable goo-wash or g-wash) is an opaque watercolor that dries to a matte or dull finish. Its high opacity allows you to paint light colors over top of dark colors. Gouache can be diluted with more water and used transparently like watercolors, although they are not quite as transparent in my opinion. They can be airbrushed or used with watercolor brushes.

When working with watercolors or other water-based paint, use two containers of water: one for cleaning paint from the brush, and one for use with the pigment. Change water often. Muddy water becomes muddy color.

The tempera paint most of you know is also a water-based paint. Plastic jars of dry tempera powder are the staple of any school art room or art cart. If care is taken when mixing, tempera can also be quite opaque. Think of it as an opaque watercolor, only a lesser quality than gouache.

By adding egg to pigment, artists of the 14th century created egg tempera. Have you ever tried to wash a plate or a fork with dried egg on it? It's not always an easy thing to do. The egg tempera dried so hard that many paintings and altarpieces are still with us today in the 21st century. Egg tempera is beautiful but probably not something you will be using in your foundation classes.

Watercolors are pigment held together with gum, which when mixed with water produces a transparent paint. It's hard to paint opaque with watercolors. Colors can be vivid when mixed properly and very soft and pastel when diluted with more water. Transparent watercolors are better for working light to dark and allowing the white of the paper to add the light to your colors.

Acrylics are a newer paint medium developed in the 20th century. They are water soluble yet dry to a waterproof plastic finish. They can be watered down and painted as transparent washes or used directly out of the tube

> When trying to apply waterbased paint to glass or plastic, try adding a drop of clear liquid dish soap to your paint. Experiment on scrap material until you get the desired amount of adhesion.

and layered on a canvas with a palette knife.

It's very important not to let acrylic paints dry in your paintbrushes. Once they do, the brush is gone. They should be cleaned as soon as you are done using them. Clean them thoroughly with soap and warm (not hot) water. Sometimes I even rinse my brushes in an ammonia-based kitchen or window cleaner, then once more with water. It's a little extra work but worth it to me.

Watercolors and gouache are available in cakes or pans of dried media waiting for water to activate them. Acrylics, like watercolors and gouache, are also available in tubes. They are sometimes sold as liquid in jars. Most paints are sold in a variety of grades, from economy to student to intermediate and then professional. You may skip a few levels when you upgrade or replace empty tubes. Most water-based paints can be used together, so as you learn what each can do, you can start to experiment with mixing them with each other.

Brushes

There are brushes for every conceivable paint and purpose. Just look in any art store or craft shop. They come in different sizes and shapes, with different types of bristles and different handle lengths.

187

Round brushes bent from being allowed to remain brush end down in the water for a prolonged period of time can be restored to original shape. Simply saturate the brush bristles or hairs with liquid soap and then wrap/roll the brush end tightly in aluminum foil, using the foil to emulate the original shape desired. Let sit and dry for a few days. Unwrap and rinse well in warm, then cool water until soap is rinsed clean. Never use hot water. It can loosen the glue that holds the bristles in the ferrule (metal part) of the brush.

The different bristles or hairs of the brush determine how much paint the brush can hold at one charging and how that paint will look when applied. The better the bristle or hair, the more expensive the brush. The more expensive the brush, the better the paint goes on the paper or canvas. The more expensive the brush, the more important it is to take good care of that brush. If you decide to study painting or illustration, don't be surprised if you find yourself looking at $200 brushes at the supply store. You may never spend that much on a brush, but be aware they can go even higher in price.

Many of you will never need anything beyond a student-grade brush while in school. The important thing to remember is that there are certain brushes for certain paints for certain marks. Use the right one. If you are not sure exactly what that should be, ask your instructor or a more experienced student who uses the same medium. The other most important thing to remember about brushes is to clean them when you are finished with them. Never leave them bristle down in a water container or jar of paint. The bristles will bend and lose their point.

Adhesives

Paste, remember paste? Good old school paste, the stuff we remember from our earliest experiences with scissors and construction paper. There was always one kid in school who ate paste. Wonder why? Some paste is made from food starch. Rice and wheat starches are often the bases for archival pastes used in collage and framing. Depending on your needs, it may be necessary to whip up a batch of rice starch. It's good for archival work or work you want to last a long time without worries of the glue staining the paper or drying out. One recipe is to combine rice starch and water, bring to boil, and then use as it cools.

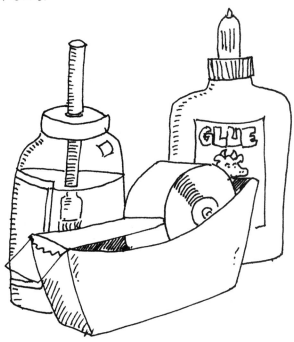

Don't be an adhesive snob just because you're in art school. Paste still has its place in the studio and does just fine when used appropriately. Paste is good for paper and some cloth. It doesn't work well with heavy objects and nonporous (very smooth, nonabsorbent) surfaces. If you are just pasting together a few scraps of paper for a rough comp or study, a regular glue stick will do fine. Glue sticks come in either permanent or releasable adhesive and are available in a variety of colors.

Like paste, glue comes in a variety of grades for use with a variety of different surfaces. Read the labels on your glue bottles. Use the right glue or you may regret it later when something falls apart. There are water-based glues and solvent-based glues.

Elmer's Glue, hide glue, and rabbit skin glue are all water based. If larger areas are to be glued together, Elmer's can be thinned down with a little water and applied to paper with a larger brush. It dries fairly quickly, so be prepared to work fast. Have your act together before you open the glue. Wash your brush out with warm (not hot) water and soap when you are finished. Hide glue is usually used when working with wood. It takes longer to dry, which comes in handy when assembling complex projects.

Not all glue is used as an adhesive. Rabbit skin glue is used for sealing raw canvas for painting. Dried rabbit skin is boiled down in water to produce a sealing agent that has been used by painters for centuries when preparing canvases for paint. After a canvas is coated with this water-based glue, oil paints will not seep through to the back.

Generally, solvent-based glues are water resistant, but they may dry out over time as the solvent base continues to evaporate. Rubber cement is solvent-based glue. Applying it to one surface and letting it dry partially or even completely before use produces a tacky gluing surface and a removable bond. Applying to both surfaces and letting the glue dry before adhering produces an almost permanent bond that only time (or rubber cement thinner) will remove.

Have you ever left a can or jar of rubber cement open for a prolonged period of time? Overnight it will become a jar of solid rubber if left opened. Even with rubber cement thinner, it will be nothing more than a jar of rubber. Close your rubber cement when you are not using it. It is also very flammable!

Spray adhesives are also flammable and should be used with care. Both permanent and removable adhesives are available in a spray can. Spray adhesives usually give a smooth, even coat of glue on the surface to which it is being applied. Take care to keep the nozzle clear, for a clog can ruin a new can. Follow the instructions on the can for cleaning the nozzle. Do not inhale the fumes, because you will be sucking glue into your sinuses and lungs. Only spray in good ventilation, preferably in a spray booth designed just for this purpose. Ask your instructors if your department has one.

SLIP-SHEETING

When mounting a piece of paper onto a board, determine exactly where you are going to place the piece you are mounting. Mark the location of the corners with reference points lightly in pencil. Make sure your rubber cement is thin enough to brush smoothly. You may need to thin your cement with rubber cement thinner. Try to get the consistency of thin pancake syrup. If you are covering a larger area, you can use a larger brush, which you can clean with rubber cement thinner. Place the piece of paper to be mounted on a clean sheet of paper, brush the rubber cement onto the back of the paper completely and quickly, brushing off and away from the edge of the paper. Do the same to the board that you are mounting the paper to. Let both surfaces dry. Test for dryness with the back of your fingers. Place a clean sheet of paper (the slip sheet) over the glued surface of the mounting board, barely leaving two of the pencil marks visible. Place the piece of paper you are mounting over the clean slip sheet. Line up the top edge of the mounting paper to the position marks on the board. When lined up,

192

burnish or rub it down. Now an inch at a time, slide out the slip sheet, burnishing the mounting sheet as you go. Continue until the slip sheet is fully removed and the top sheet is smoothly adhered to the mounting board.

Scotch tape, masking tape, drafting tape, double-sided tape, artists' tape, and kraft tape are each designed for a specific use as shown in the following list:

- ✔ Scotch or cellophane tape. Clear plastic for use on paper.
- ✔ Masking tape. A coated tan or beige paper; use on many smooth dry surfaces.
- ✔ Drafting tape. A coated tan or beige paper; removes cleanly from paper.
- ✔ Artists' tape. Similar to drafting tape; smooth white paper that can be drawn on.
- ✔ Kraft tape. Brown kraft paper, water activated; used to stretch watercolor paper.
- ✔ Double-sided tape. For presentation and display work; also used in framing.

Depending on your needs you will find permanent and removable adhesives available in most of these tapes. Most are also available in a variety of widths and roll sizes.

If you do not have a tape dispenser, keep your tape when not in use in a ziplock bag to keep the sides of the tape clean from dirt, dust, and lint. When you pull that first roll of funky tape from the bottom of your backpack you will know what I mean.

From the age-old glue made by boiling animal hides to the humble back-to-school plastic bottle, glues and adhesives have been a part of our studio supplies for a long time. The secret is knowing what they are good for and when to use them. Knowing what thins or breaks them down and cleans them up is equally important.

You may find times that a hot glue gun from the craft store is what you need. Don't forget that staples, brass fasteners, or even a needle and thread can be the adhesive you seek. Assess your needs and what you are trying to accomplish, then pick the right adhesive. Using the proper one will help you keep your project together as much or as little as you desire.

Things That Cut

The tools that you use in your foundation classes and tools that you use in your major classes may differ greatly. Buy scissors based on your needs. You may never need a $30 pair of scissors, but if you had them you'd be able to tell the difference between them and a less expensive pair. If you've never shopped for scissors before, it can be an eye-opening experience. Use scissors with longer blades to make longer, smoother cuts. Take care of scissors, keep them clean and only use them for the materials they were designed to cut.

Don't use scissors to cut illustration board. You'll trash the board, your fingers, and the scissors. When cutting board, try using a utility knife or an X-Acto-type razor knife. Always start with a new sharp blade and remember to let the blade do the cutting. The more pressure you put on the blade, the less control you have of it. Loss of control equals cut fingers. Keep control. Keep fingers.

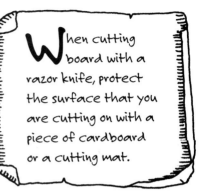

When cutting board with a razor knife, protect the surface that you are cutting on with a piece of cardboard or a cutting mat.

When making long cuts on board, use a metal straight-edge and a sharp knife. Making many lighter passes of the knife over the board will give you a nice clean cut. Be sure to measure first, then double-check your measurement. When it's right, hold your straightedge down firmly and guide your blade along the edge, the entire length of the cut if possible. Repeat this in a smooth and deliberate manner. Take your time, it is not a race.

A razor blade knife is only as good as the blade in it. Make sure you have extras on hand. When they stop cutting smooth and start to catch or drag a little when cutting, it's time to change them. If you are on your last blade and it's dull, try running the edge of the blade against a piece of fine sandpaper a few times. That may help hone the edge and allow you one more clean cut.

When disposing of old blades, be careful where you put them. Don't leave them lying around and don't just toss them into the trashcan. Wrap a piece of masking tape around the blade before you toss it, or keep a jar just for old blades that you will recycle later. Be careful—cuts from old rusty blades, even if they don't need stitches, should probably be followed with a tetanus shot.

It's a good idea to have a sharp pocketknife in your art box for working on location or sharpening a pencil. You may want to check school policy on whether it would be considered a weapon. No need to stir up trouble even if unintentionally.

Paper

Paper is also available in a variety of sizes and grades. Like a brush, there is a proper paper for each medium. Paper is available in tablets or pads, as single sheets, and in rolls. You might have an extensive knowledge of paper or you might know next to nothing. Much depends on your previous art education and how much time you have spent in your local art supply store.

The papers and boards you work with in the first-year courses are usually specified by the instructor and on the syllabus you received for the class. There is a reason for the type suggested so use what is specified. Watercolor paper absorbs water without disintegrating; plate bristol takes a smooth line nicely; marker paper accepts marker with minimal bleeding; newsprint accepts charcoal well and is economical, which is good for drawing courses where you may use 10 sheets per class. Whatever paper you are using, look at the paper the students around you are using. They may have a different brand, color, or finish than you. Ask them about the paper, how it holds up to erasing or water. Does it take paint well? You will find your own preferences.

196

Paper comes in all grades, from the inexpensive to the ridiculous. Use what is appropriate. Don't use a $9 piece of rag watercolor paper for your first watercolor painting, but be sure to use watercolor paper. If you stay with watercolor as a medium or even as something just for yourself on the side, you will know when you are ready to move up to the good stuff. The same is true with most papers. You will also find that papers with cotton or rag fibers in them are stronger and take more punishment. Like most anything else, with paper you get what you pay for. Knowing what to buy can be confusing. Take a trip down the paper aisle of your art supply store.

SCRAPS

An instructor of mine once handed out small 1 X 2 inch pieces of watercolor paper. Everyone in the class got four or five of them. Each was a different weight and finish of watercolor paper. Just seeing and feeling the difference between them was an eye-opening experience. Until then my knowledge of watercolor paper was little more than knowing that there was such a thing and it came in tablets and sheets.

DIGITAL ART TOOLS

So many majors require computer skills these days that after the foundation classes, some students may never touch a brush or marker again. The remainder of their studio coursework will be done with computers and other digital tools. Others may rarely use a computer for a creative tool. Either way, they are here, and at least for the time being, you should take advantage of the technology when you can. This doesn't mean to throw away the traditional tools of the artist, just be aware and in tune with the digital tools that can expand your creativity.

If your major is heavily involved with digital technology, you should be prepared to spend extra hours learning software updates before you can work smoothly with them. Software packages have major updates about once a year. Besides investing the time to learn the new tools, you may also have to pay for them. Remember, after you buy your computer, you have to buy software for it. It's good to get in the habit of buying software and owning legitimate licensed versions of the tools of your trade. Besides being illegal, copied software is not guaranteed to be stable and free of viruses. Would you want your doctor to be using a cracked copy of software when running tests on you or your loved ones?

It would be futile to try to include a list of technology that wouldn't be outdated or even obsolete by the time this book is printed. So you should stay aware of the advancing technology in your chosen field.

FINDING THE TOOLS

When you are ready to purchase a computer, check with your department chair or college bookstore for any special student discounts or programs that might be available. You might even inquire directly to the manufacturer of the computer in which you are interested. Whether you buy online or at the mall, save your receipts. If there is one thing I have learned over the years, it is to save your receipts in case of a problem. Keep them somewhere safe where you can find them.

When buying supplies from a catalog, look for quantity discounts. Check with your classmates who might want to go in on a larger order.

When shopping for art supplies, start with your school bookstore. It is ordering stock based on the school curriculum. If you have to look elsewhere for something, check the phonebook. If you need something at once, are you prepared to drive an hour? You may have to. If you have a few days you can also buy online or by catalog. Many places ship next day freight or overnight delivery if requested.

However you get your supplies, just make sure you have them for class. Be prepared. Don't fail a class because you don't have the tools. Take care of your supplies and equipment and they will last for years. If you do, when you set up your next studio after graduation you will have a good solid starting set of the tools of your trade.

Notes:

Pythian Sybil Bronze, Marcello, 1836

CHAPTER

Setting Up Your Studio

- ✔ Establish a Place to Work
- ✔ Living Alone or Sharing Spaces
- ✔ Organizing Your Supplies
- ✔ Furniture
- ✔ Light, Electric, Ventilation
- ✔ Feng Shui

When you start school, you will find that it isn't always easy to gather all of your supplies together to go into a school studio to do your homework. There may be times that you have no choice. Perhaps there is special equipment or technology that you must use, perhaps it's a large project and you need the space. But what about when you can work at home? Do you have a place set aside for your studio? Are you living with new roommates? Do they need studio space? You'll have homework projects before you know it. First give some thought to your needs and then some thought as to what is realistic. Find a happy medium you can live with and then get yourself a space that you can work in without causing a riot. Remember you may have to share space with family, friends, or roommates.

Establish a Place to Work

As you prepare to start school it is important to have a comfortable place to work. The sooner that you establish a place to work, a place that artwork can be left undisturbed until the next work session, the easier it will be to get your work done on time and to keep your supplies together.

The studio area you set up will vary depending on your major, living conditions, and quarters. If you are living at home, you may already have a room or area set up. That is a great start, but you may still need to adjust your room or area to get the maximum use out of the space.

Do not do your homework on the kitchen table unless you absolutely have to. And if you have no other choice,

202

clean it off before you start work and clear your work as soon as you are finished. Have you ever put a piece of paper down on the kitchen table only to pick it up to find a greasy butter stain on it or that there was water on the table and your paper now has a water stain on it? The kitchen table is located in the kitchen and we all know that the kitchen is a comfortable room. But it is also the table from which we eat and, in some cases, on which we prepare food.

When doing your homework, studio work, or written work, avoid the kitchen. It is a place where bad things can happen to your work.

Avoid eating where you work. That may seem almost impossible to do. But use caution when you do eat where you work. An accident can happen anytime in anyplace. It is too easy to spill food or drink on your work or equipment.

203

Even a small drop of water will mar a gouache painting; a splash of soda can trash a computer keyboard. Use the kitchen table for eating and your work area for working.

When you have art projects to work on, it is better to divide your time, working in shorter sessions on a piece.

Try to keep food and drink away from projects. Glasses can sweat in warm weather, causing an unwanted dripping problem.

Smaller segments of time might mean having a piece of artwork out on the table for a number of days. The kitchen and the table found there are high traffic areas and not the appropriate places to leave artwork. You will need to establish a studio space that is used just for that—studio work.

Wash hands with soap and dry totally before working on a project, especially after eating. Oils from foods or your own skin easily transfer onto paper causing paints to transfer unevenly.

Living Alone or Sharing Spaces

Like anything else, there are pros and cons to living alone. To start with, there are no compatibility issues. Pro. There is also no companionship or camaraderie. Con. But thinking of the cons can be pessimistic and not the state of mind we are looking for here. Let's look at the pros instead and the positive side of living alone. It is an opportunity to set up your studio and living space just the way you want. If there is a party or loud music, it's only when you say so. When you want to sleep, you can. There is no waiting for the bathroom.

If you are living at home, look at your room. Can you make it the space you now need it to be? Maybe you can with just a few minor additions or deletions. If you are sharing the room with another family member, can you change that situation? You will be clocking some late night hours. You may need to check out the basement or attic space. Don't be afraid to grab a broom or invest a few hours putting a coat of paint on the walls.

Some furniture or memorabilia may need to go into storage—stuff you want to keep for one reason or another but don't really need or have room for right now.

Label your boxes well. You may need some of those things occasionally so you should be able to locate them with relative ease.

Do not work with sprays or dirty, dusty materials in the same room as your computer. If you must, then be sure to cover the computer (also your stereo and TV) with a towel or some other piece of cloth. You will thank yourself for doing so later. Depending on your major or choice of media, you may need a workshop separate from your studio or computer area. If you have to work with computers and electronic equipment as well as paint or clay or aerosols, do your best to keep them apart. Hanging old blankets or rugs from the ceiling in a basement can divide a large space into smaller rooms. In the basement studio I have seen bed sheets stapled to the ceiling rafters to keep the dirt from falling onto computers. The studio kind of looked like a big tent. A small closet filled with shelves can become a workstation. Each shelf holds a computer component. A printer, a keyboard, a monitor, each has a shelf. Simply open the closet, roll up a chair, and voila, a workspace. A work area that takes zero floor space. You don't have to frame out walls and hang drywall to establish a new or separate room.

Be comfortable in your space. If you need certain creature comforts to be productive, go ahead and add them. Music, TV, fridge—use 'em if you got 'em. Just don't spoil yourself so much that you can't work unless the extreme conditions are met.

Sharing Space

Are you sharing the living and studio space with others? Are their needs the same as yours? A good place to begin is by getting together and talking. All of the parties involved should agree on how the space will be utilized best. In the dorm, apartment, or even a house setting, there are a number of different options to explore. Obviously the more room you have to work with, the easier it will be. If space is at a premium, you may have to be a bit more inventive. In one of my studios, I converted a small walk-in hallway closet to a darkroom. In another house, I stapled sheets to the basement ceiling to keep the area dust free. Just remember that each person in the area should have a say. After all two or three or six creative minds in one space . . . the possibilities are endless . . . the possibilities are frightening. If more than one solution is feasible or interesting, try each one. Give each idea a chance. You will have to fine-tune along the way. That's OK. It is part of the process. Try not to change things right before midterms or finals. Make sure you have time to troubleshoot obstacles in your plan.

Having a common living area and separate sleep and work areas always gives a large area for eating, entertaining, and relaxing. Set up your studio and your sleep area together. Your apartment or dorm may already have furniture. Decide what you need and either put the rest in storage or trade to other roommates.

Creating a loft sleep/work area is a great way to take full advantage of your space. By setting up your bed as a loft above your work area, you economize the footprint

208

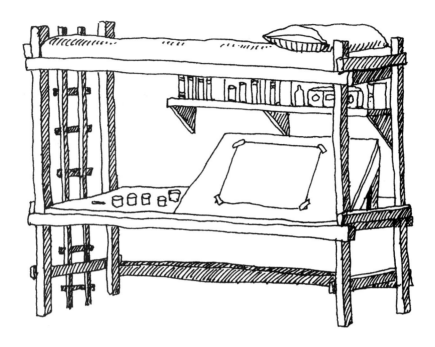

of your area. Under the raised bed you can set up your desk and drawing table. If you plan it well, you can put up shelves to accommodate your supplies. A shelf attached to the bottom of your bed is a handy place to store flat artwork. Use paper portfolios to protect and sort work. You will need lighting as well. Be careful not to use lights that require high wattage. One-hundred-watt bulbs can emit a lot of heat and even be a fire hazard. Fluorescent lights give off less heat but the light is not as pleasing. More on lighting later in this chapter.

When leaving a project on a drawing board or table for a number of days while working on it, cover it with a sheet of clean inexpensive paper such as news-print between sessions.

209

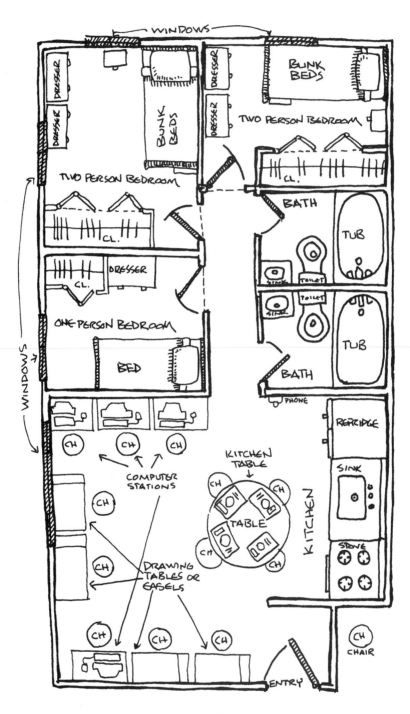

If two people share a bedroom, bunk beds offer another way to maximize space. Of course someone will have to take the top bunk. Making bunk arrangements will leave space for studio furniture. Again if you share the space with another, it is important to be mindful of his or her needs both for work and sleep. Again shelving can keep supplies and tools together.

The common living area can also be used for studio space. I have seen students in an apartment put all of their drawing tables, easels, and computer tables in the main living room area, pooling their resources and leaving their sleeping quarters for sleep and privacy. When the work area is common, it is important to respect the work and tools of your roommates. If you borrow something, return it the way you got it. Clean a brush, replace a dull blade when you're done. Avoid using someone else's computer if possible. Who will be responsible if it crashes? And if it does, is the work backed up? If it is necessary to share a computer, get yourself a separate storage system; external high-speed hard drives are plentiful and reasonably priced. By connecting and disconnecting your hard drive when you are done, your work is somewhat safe if the computer dies. Please take the time and effort to run virus protection software. More on this subject in Chapter 10.

CO-OPS AND SHARING SPACES AND EXPENSES

The practice of sharing workspaces is not a new idea or one unique to students. Co-ops or cooperatives have been used for years. Two or three people can share the expense of a larger or nicer studio. Maybe a nicer location or larger space is desired. Pooling of funds is an example of the old adage, there's strength in numbers.

211

EARL'S FILLING STATION

In high school I worked at a gas station. A mechanic I knew made a deal with the owner of the station. During the weeknights he would keep the gas station open from 11 p.m. until 7 a.m. He would also pay some rent to the owner. In return he got use of the garage bays to do mechanical work on Volkswagens. It was a small town and there were few mechanics who knew how to work on VWs. The owner got more business. The mechanic got business and a place to work. The town got another place to get their beetles worked on. The two shared the expense and both benefited by the union.

When I opened my first studio outside of my home, I began by renting two small rooms above a department store. I was doing architectural illustration and t-shirt printing. Well, the screen printing side of the business grew and before I knew it I needed more space. After about a year, another office space consisting of five rooms and a powder room became available on the same floor of the building. I needed space but not that much. I

212

decided to rent it, but I also decided to start a type of a co-op. I rented one-room studios to other artists. We all shared in the expense of the telephone and other utilities. We took messages for one another. Even did jobs for each other. We all got a better space together than we could have alone. Whether in school or out of school, a co-op can give you added buying or renting power. Sharing space has its pros and cons. Be sure to explore the idea when setting up a studio.

ORGANIZING YOUR SUPPLIES

Keeping your studio organized is not always an easy task. You may need help. My wife is good at helping me sort and organize stuff. Some people are neat. They come by it naturally. Some people are slobs. This condition can be inherited or a reactionary reflex. Either way, keeping your workplace in some level of order is a good thing and something you should take seriously, whether you put stuff away immediately after use or have a weekly cleanup session. Perhaps straightening up at the end of a project works for you. Try to get in the habit of cleaning and putting away your supplies where they belong when you're finished using them. The important thing is that you have a place to put stuff when you are done with it. The same place each time. Check out any of the many Dollar Stores for storage solutions. There are also stores that only sell containers of all sizes. Whether you are storing paints or CD-ROMs, it is important to be able to find them when you need them.

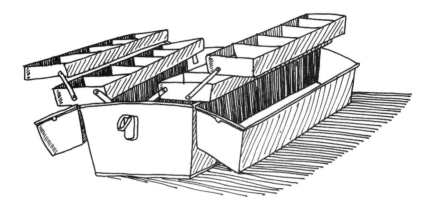

Fishing tackle boxes and tool boxes also work well for storage. I have a small box for charcoals, a slightly larger one for watercolors and gouache, another for acrylic, still another for airbrush stuff, and a larger three-drawer steel box for my good brushes, knives, scissors, and tape. I keep them all (except the steel three-drawer) in an old trunk. It's a great way to keep supplies organized and together.

Like the tackle box for paints, I have portfolio binders with sleeves of prints and CDs and a briefcase for my laptop computer and external digital storage drive. Many of the same ideas that work for traditional supplies will work with your digital supplies.

Keep Band-Aids, aspirin, a pack of matches, and a few dollars of change in your paint or tool box. You never know when you'll need them and they don't take up that much space.

Have a folder or envelope in a safe place for your important school papers such as signed agreements, receipts, tuition bills, grades, and so on. It is easy for these papers to vanish or be eaten by the mountains of junk mail that invade our lives. Deal with this problem from the beginning. Have a drawer or file cabinet for them. You'll be glad you did when you need any of your school records.

Dressers are good for storage. Use different drawers for different supplies. Avoid throwing just anything in just any drawer. Tablets and paper go in one drawer, paints in another, brushes in another, pencils and pens in another, and so on. Old furniture is often left behind when people move. It doesn't matter where it comes from. Thrift shops or Ikea, a chest of drawers can keep your supplies together.

FURNITURE

Some of the furniture in your studio can be old stuff from the attic or yard sale finds, and some will be more specifically designed as studio furniture. Such pieces may be more of an investment, but well worth it. When the spring semester or session is ending, watch for students selling drawing tables and chairs. Not everyone will be returning to school. Some will graduate, some will drop out, some will upgrade, and some will simply want to travel and be rid of it. Either way, watch the bulletin boards at school.

The Table

You will need a few tables to have an effective work space. A large table, maybe another smaller table. You may need a flat table. Old kitchen tables, desks, or doors on saw horses or milk crates work fine. Adjustable drawing tables are great too. Usually these can be set or adjusted by height and pitch of tabletop. They come in a variety of sizes and vary from economical to executive in cost. A smaller side table for supplies currently being

216

used is also good to have. You may need yet another
table or desk for your computer. Just be aware that tables
can easily become places where stuff accumulates. Old
sketches, research material, even junk mail has a
tendency to pile up on tables.

The Chair

Your chair should be comfortable and ergonomic. If at all
possible, do not scrimp on your chair. You will spend many
hours on it and those hours will be much easier if you

have a good chair. Chairs have come down in price over the years. There are some good deals if you shop. Don't buy one just because it's cheap, for that is what you will probably get. If you shop, you can find one that will serve you well through your school days for about $150 to $200.

AND IT FIT JUST RIGHT

My first decent chair cost me about $150 and lasted me about 10 years. When it came time to replace it, I didn't shop for comfort; I shopped for price and availability. After about a year I couldn't take it anymore. I hated that chair I bought. Even though it was adjustable, it just wasn't comfortable to me. After getting paid for a freelance job, I decided to get a new chair. I shopped and must have tried 15 chairs at three or four stores. I even went back and forth between two stores to try chairs again. I had budgeted $400. I finally bought the one that fit me best. Ironically it cost under $200. That was about four years ago. I can sit in this chair (I'm sitting in it now) all day and not be uncomfortable.

The other day I walked into my studio and my chair had been replaced by my daughter's chair. I panicked. Where was my chair? Turns out she wanted to try it for a while. Can't say that I blame her, it's a great chair. But for that brief moment of panic I was reminded just how important a good chair is.

You will eventually need and acquire other furniture. The style and expense will depend on your tastes and budget. Think function. Bookcases, desks, and flat files are all great investment values. Flat files provide a safe place for paper, canvas, finished artwork,

Have both trash and recycling containers in your work space. You may even have one just for paper.

prints, and other items. They are available from art supply and even some business supply stores. They are very reasonable from online auctions, but they are big. Shipping costs may undo any real savings. Shop around. I have a set of chestnut flat map files from the roundhouse of the old Reading Railroad Terminal in Philadelphia. I bought them at an architectural salvage yard.

Light, Electric, Ventilation

Power

Consider power, lighting, and ventilation. Will there be an issue with these? You require additional power for computers and other electronic equipment. Don't risk an electrical fire. Don't overload the circuits. Use power strips for surge protection, but don't plug one into another and then max them both out unless you know for a fact that the outlet you are plugging all of this expensive equipment into can handle the demand.

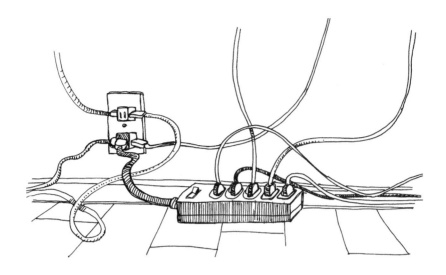

Ventilation

Will you or your roommate being using media that gives off fumes? Airbrushes used to be a common tool for the illustration student. Today few people use them, but there are times when you may need to or choose to. When working with an airbrush, you should be aware ventilation is required with its use. Also depending on the type of paint you use, the fumes produced can be flammable. Even oil paints give off fumes that can make some people nauseous. Do not be fooled by using oil paint thinners that smell like citrus. They still give off fumes, although may not as disagreeable, but ventilation should still be used. Sometimes a window is enough or even a kitchen exhaust fan. Sometimes an inexpensive window fan can be put in the window to either bring in fresh air or take out the fumes. Do not use lacquer-based paints in your room or apartment if you can help it. The fumes they give off can be extremely flammable and can make you sick.

221

READ THE WARNING LABEL!

When I was in college, I did a lot of different odd jobs and freelance work. Signs were among the long list. Anything from showcards to banners to wooden outdoor signs with lighting. One particular job I landed was from a local gas station who wanted me to repaint an outdoor metal sign. It already had a frame and was very sturdy. My job was to repaint it with a different message. No problem. In fact the garage even supplied me with the paint. They had a particular color in mind and with their experience doing bodywork on cars, they felt that lacquer spray paint would be a good base to start with. Of course all I thought was, hey, I don't have to go get paint, great.

Well, I sanded the metal to roughen the surface and when it came time to paint it, the weather was bad, so down to the basement I went and into the outer room. I knew enough to close the door to keep the fumes in the room and not let them spread through the house. But I didn't think the fumes would be as strong as they were. The room (with no ventilation) filled with a yellow haze and even though I was wearing a paper mask, I soon began to feel the effects of the paint. Luckily, I was almost done, so I finished spraying and left the room, closing the door behind me.

I went to visit my girlfriend and progressively felt sicker. I spent a short amount of time with her until it got so bad that I had to ask her to drive me home. Alas, I was driving a 1962 MG midget and she did not know how to drive a stick. None of her roommates could either. I had to leave. I made it out of her dorm and to the side of the building where I fell to the ground and lay under a bush in the rain for what seemed to be hours. When I finally felt well enough to drive, I returned home vowing I would never use lacquer paint again without the proper ventilation.

Lighting

Have you ever gotten dressed inside and walked out into the sunlight to discover that what you were wearing didn't match anymore? Choosing colors in different types of light can be tricky. So can mixing colors, especially for your color theory class. You may want to position your drawing table or easel near a window where you can get natural sunlight. Some people mix different types of lighting. There was a time when I had a fluorescent

223

fixture above my drawing table with one cool and one warm tube in it. They each give off a different tone of light. Then on either side of the table I had arm lamps with incandescent bulbs, 60 or 75 watts. I tried 100-watt bulbs once, but they got too hot and burned out the switches of my lamps. If your lamp has a warning sticker limiting the size of bulb to use, heed the warning. Do not risk the hazard of a fire.

When setting up your drawing table, computer table, desk, or easel, try not to position it where you will have a ceiling fixture or lamp behind you, casting your own shadow onto your work. When setting up your computer table, diffused lighting is preferred. Bounce light off of walls. A defused light behind your computer monitor keeps glare from reflecting on your screen. A good solution for computer lighting is to have diffused track lighting on a dimmer switch and a small task light at your table for reading your reference material. But you have to decide just how important lighting is to you and what you can afford.

FENG SHUI

Feng shui has been practiced for thousands of years. To the layperson the basic idea of feng shui concerns the energy that flows in our lives and where we live them. It deals with the placement of furniture and other objects in our lives. Have you ever noticed how some architectural spaces or rooms feel more inviting than others do? The removal of clutter helps the energy flow. Something as simple as the direction a building is facing can change how it is received by people.

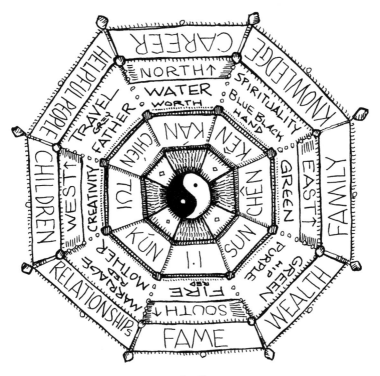

225

After reading a little on the subject but really not knowing much about it, I decided to investigate. From the information readily available to the consumer public, I found enough to be dangerous yet informed. On paper I tried a few floor plans and then eventually rearranged my studio. The simple adjustment of a desk made a noticeable difference. Keeping it neat and orderly helps. Of course, the clutter always seems to rear its ugly head in my studio. But once I regroup and straighten up, my studio becomes a very comfortable space to work in.

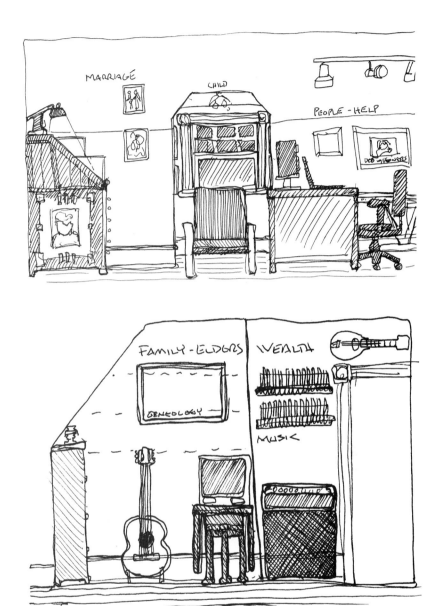

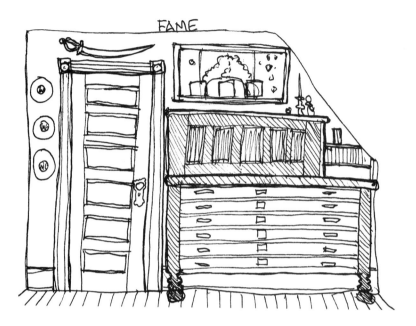

Glenn Groves is a certified practitioner in the tradition of Tibetan tantric Buddhism. He completed three years of training with Melani Lewandowski, feng shui master who received the teachings from world-renowned master Lin Yun Rinpoche. He has shared with me the following information: "Feng shui is a fundamental component of Chinese medicine. It is the energetic science of creating spaces with the intention of inviting the greatest good to fill our homes, work spaces, and lives. This is accomplished by directing the energy, or chi, through the conscious placement of objects in the environment. The term _feng shui_ means wind and water. It comes from the symbolic concept that people flourish where the winds are gentle and water plentiful."

You may have to compromise. You may want to place a piece of furniture in one spot for its lighting, but the

228

best spot according to this methodology is deep in the shadows. Try to find the balance. You can always rearrange later if you don't like it. Some people are open to this practice, some think it is a bunch of Eastern mumbo-jumbo. It makes sense to me. I've tried it. You can decide for yourself.

Glenn also recommended two books worth reading if you decide to take this approach when setting up your studio or work space. Look for <u>Feng Shui: Harmony by Design</u> by Nancy Santo Pietro, Perigee Books, 1996, and <u>Interior Design with Feng Shui</u> by Sarah Rossbach, Arkana, 1991.

NOTES:

Starry Night, Vincent Van Gogh, 1889

CHAPTER

The Digital Chapter

- ✔ Working with Digital Media
- ✔ Backing Up Files
- ✔ Advancing Technology
- ✔ Organizing
- ✔ Health Issues

Because technology is changing so fast, this chapter deals more with the principles of working with digital technologies than with specific items and brand names of the day. The important thing to remember when using these tools is that you have the ability to make backup copies of your work. Because the tools are machines and the possibility of failure exists, it is your responsibility to have not only backed up files but a backup plan as well. What will you do if the unthinkable happens?

WORKING WITH DIGITAL MEDIA

Majoring in art does not exclude you from using digital technology. Chances are you will. Whether it's a computer to type a paper on, a three-dimensional scanner to digitize a clay study, or a PDA to keep track of your homework, in today's society it's almost inevitable. You probably already are working with it in some shape or form.

Some of you will choose an art major in which the computer will be your primary tool. For others it may be nothing more than a convenience. If you use it wisely, it can save you hours of work and even open new creative directions for your work. If you are careless, the results can be devastating.

BACKING UP FILES

In my opinion the most important lessons to remember are save often and backup your files. If the technology you are using experiences a power surge, interruption, or failure, all current work will be lost. If work is saved every

232

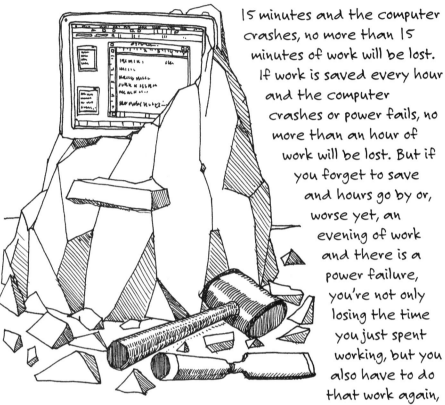

15 minutes and the computer crashes, no more than 15 minutes of work will be lost. If work is saved every hour and the computer crashes or power fails, no more than an hour of work will be lost. But if you forget to save and hours go by or, worse yet, an evening of work and there is a power failure, you're not only losing the time you just spent working, but you also have to do that work again, taking time from another task. Many software applications have settings that perform periodic backups. Use them. Don't forget to back up on a portable medium such as a CD-R or a DVD.

Saving while you work can protect that work only so much. But what happens if the media to which you save your work (floppy disk, CD-R, DVD, or hard drive) fails? After all, floppies and CDs are mass produced. Really mass produced. Quality control can only catch so much. In addition, equipment gets old, there are power blackouts, lightning strikes, and viruses. If the hard drive on your computer dies, there is no guarantee that anything on it will survive. The smart thing to do is to have a backup of

233

your files separate from the computer. Back up your files, make a second copy. Make the effort to back up work on a regular basis. If your computer died right now ask yourself, How much would I lose? Could I get by or would I be crushed?

When you back up your work, try to find a place to keep those files that is separate from your original files. Your

hard drive should never be your only backup. Maybe you give them to a friend to hold. Depending on how important they are, maybe you will keep them in a school locker, maybe a bank safety deposit box. Are you saving and protecting a term paper or a doctoral thesis? If your backups are stored with your originals and there is a catastrophic event such as a fire or accident, it's all gone. But if your backups are elsewhere, you may be all right. You can be as carefree or as prudent as you like. It is up to you. Just remember that some day when something happens to your files, and that day will likely come, you will either feel extreme frustration or extreme relief.

Never use school equipment as the only backup of your work. Many schools have routine maintenance scheduled for their computers that may include reformatting hard drives. Reformatting is erasing, gone, kaput, history! This can leave your work vulnerable. If your files are small enough or text files, you may simply e-mail them to yourself and not open the e-mail. Have a set of backup files on the e-mail server. Your school will probably offer you server space and e-mail. There are many free e-mail services as well as inexpensive ones. Take advantage of them. But don't count on anything as exclusive, absolute protection. Manufactured products wear out, break, or eventually become obsolete.

ADVANCING TECHNOLOGY

Between new advances in hardware development and the never-ending stream of new software releases and updates, trying to stay current with technology can be a some-what futile experience. But once you start trying, it can be hard to stop. If the technology is a tool of your profession, it will be a necessity.

Budgeting

Some people budget a car payment into their monthly expenses. They want the reliability, comfort, status, and maybe even the peace of mind that can come with driving a new car. Computers and other high-tech gadgets can be thought of the same. Don't forget to include software upgrades in your budget if the computer plays an important role in your major. If you figure you will always need it, it may be easier to stay current with technology if it is always part of your budget. Some computer companies offer trade-in or upgrade packages and promotions. Again the studio major you choose may affect how deep into technology you dive and how much of your wallet it embraces.

236

When to Buy a Computer and What to Buy

Is it necessary to buy a computer when starting school? The answer depends on a number of things. Your school may require not only that you have a new computer with certain software, it may even specify the brand and model. The school may provide computers sufficient for your needs during the first few semesters or foundation year. Then you purchase one for the lion's share of your assignments outside of class. You may even go through your entire schooling not owning a computer at all, using only what the school supplies. Each case is a little different.

Some of the big retail stores offer back-to-school specials, then holiday shopping specials, then there are the after holiday clearance sales. If you watch the Sunday papers, you will always be able to find something. Do not forget that there are stores on the Internet offering great deals. Some are specifically geared toward schools and students. Maybe you can save the sales tax; maybe there is free shipping. It does not take long to do a search. Don't forget to check with your school bookstore or technology department for educational packages that might be offered direct from the manufacturer to your school. If you work on an Apple computer, you should check out Apple Computer's educational sales area on the Apple Web site.

Before you buy, be sure to check with your department as to what software and hardware are recommended for your program of study. While many artists favor a Macintosh, many computer animators prefer a PC. Not all applications are available on both platforms. Both have

237

much to offer. You may even end up with one of each. Be sure to get one with sufficient power and storage for your needs. Some hardware can be upgraded, allowing for future expansion and an extended life.

ORGANIZING

Having all this great technology at your disposal is cool. Being able to learn it and work with it is very cool. The art that can be created with it is very, very cool. Not being able to find your homework, project, or thesis undoes it all.

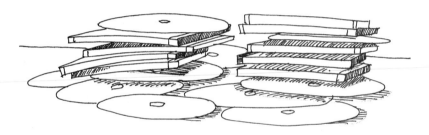

Some people are untidy and messy; some are so organized that it hurts. Everyone else is somewhere in between. One thing all should pay attention to is how organized they keep their digital media and files, including all backup work. Don't be afraid to hold on to your files for awhile. Even older files and software versions should be retained. They don't take up that much space, and today storage is much more affordable than it has been in the past. Try to have some sort of order or a system. Will you keep your removable media (disks, CDs, and so forth) in wallets, boxes, drawers? Any number of storage systems are available. You may even have your own idea of how to keep it together. Just make it a point to always know where your files are. Try to copy important files from old media to new media formats before the hardware for the older media is no longer commercially available or has become obsolete.

To eliminate much confusion in the future, be sure to label and date all work. If the work is confidential you may password-protect it or even encrypt the documents. Remember to keep backup copies of work in a separate location or with someone your trust.

THE PRICE OF PROTECTION

Before the introduction and availability of recordable CDs, a computer artist working since the mideighties would have seen and probably used three, four, even five different types of storage media. There were $5\frac{1}{4}$ inch floppy disks, $3\frac{1}{2}$ inch floppy disks both double density and high density, Bernoulli, SyQuest, Zip, and Jaz cartridges, all available in different sizes at different costs. It was not unheard of for a professional artist to have a library of 20 to 30 zip disks (cost: $15 each), and 10 to 20 SyQuest

(continued)

carts (cost: $100 to $150 each depending on size), each requiring a different drive costing anywhere from $100 to $500. Of course, these all became obsolete and small fortunes were spent to back up work. Even the first commercially available CD burners cost thousands of dollars.

While the expense of backing up work has decreased, the importance of backing up the work is as crucial as ever. Today there is no excuse for not having your work backed up. The work itself is the investment and should be protected.

HEALTH ISSUES

Health issues? What health issues? It's not like working with a band saw or molten metal. But think of the workout your eyes and wrists are getting. Carpal tunnel syndrome is almost a rite of passage for today's Web designer. Have you ever noticed that it's the digital artists who are wearing those cutting-edge eyeglasses? It is not always just a fashion statement; many times it is a necessity.

If you are going to be spending long hours in front of a computer, be sure to have a comfortable chair that is ergonomically adjustable. After all, a six-foot tall person and a five-foot tall person will have different preferences to the height of their chair and table. Everyone wants to be comfortable in his or her work environment.

Lighting should be diffused or indirect, placed so it does not reflect onto your monitor. Somewhere to the side or behind the monitor is good. Have a smaller task light available for books and other reference work when working on the computer.

Stretch your eyes every now and then. Get up from your chair and walk around. Look out a window, down the street, or across the room. Stretch your arms and back as well. This doesn't have to be a workout, just a quick extension of limbs and torso. It only takes seconds and while the relief may not seem a big deal at the time, if you do not stretch every now and then, the accumulated hours can lead to tight muscles and tension headaches.

Don't forget your life away from school. The things that you do there can affect your work in the studio. Don't be foolish or careless when working with power tools, mechanical devices, glass, fire, and solvents. Protect your eyes, your hands, yourself. Don't take unnecessary risks.

242

NOTES:

243

Study of Dancer, Henri Toulouse Lautrec, 1891

CHAPTER

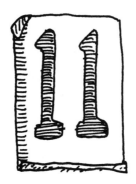

Miscellaneous Stuff

- ✔ Measuring
- ✔ Basic One-, Two-, and Three-Point Perspective
- ✔ Hand Lettering
- ✔ Setting Up a Picture Library
- ✔ Finding Research Materials and Inspiration
- ✔ When Traveling
- ✔ Real World and Virtual Places

Trying to include in this book every topic that will get you through school is unrealistic because each of you is a different person, a different artist, and you will all experience school in different ways. Even trying to cover just some of the basics, I have discovered that there are pieces that just do not warrant an entire chapter. Some advice and information did not fit into the different categories in this book. So here is a chapter dedicated to miscellaneous stuff.

MEASURING

In this age of digital devices, some students have actually grown up not learning how to tell time on an analog clock. Some students from overcrowded inner city schools or poor rural areas may have grown up not learning how to read a ruler. Measuring, reading a ruler, even telling time all seem like tasks that should be second nature, but this is not always true. Learning must be reinforced with practical application. If this does not occur, the lesson is forgotten. For those who may not have learned, and those who may have forgotten, here are a few helpful measuring tools.

246

Reading a Ruler

When measuring with a ruler, try to use one in decent condition. If the end is worn and rounded, the measurement might not be accurate. Stainless steel rulers generally do not have those problems. Rulers built into software applications never wear down but are only useful when measuring on the computer. Sometimes you just need to measure a physical object. So when you pick up a ruler, be sure you know how it works.

Your major may dictate what type of ruler you will use; inches, meters, and picas are all units of measure used in the arts. As a result you may have more than one ruler in your studio. Knowing how to use them properly is of the utmost importance.

If the back of your ruler is cork and it gets dirty, that dirt can spread to your project when working. Try putting masking tape over top of the cork, running the length of the ruler. Two strips will usually do the trick.

Most of the world outside of the United States uses the metric system of measuring. You have probably been introduced to it in school. It may have been a few years ago, and you might not have even thought about it since then. But if you work outside of the U.S. or do work with overseas companies, you might just want to brush up on your metric system.

The metric system is based on the decimal system of counting using the power of ten. It is based on the meter and subdivisions of the meter in increments of ten. This eliminates the need to calculate and convert fractions. The scientific community has long used the metric system of measuring. The metric ruler divides the meter into one hundred equal parts known as centimeters. Each centimeter is divided into ten equal parts known as millimeters. Knowing that there are 100 centimeters in a meter, and 10 millimeters in a single centimeter, tells us that there are 1000 millimeters in a meter.

A ruler used when working with type is divided into points and picas as the units of measure. There are 12 points in a pica and 6 picas in an inch. This equates to 72 points in an inch. Points are more often used to measure and indicate the height of a letter and picas are more often used to indicate the length of a line of type.

If the ruler is based on feet and inches, there are 12 inches in a foot and each inch is divided into fractions of an inch. The longest hash marks are at the beginning of each inch, usually accompanied by the number. Each inch is divided in half, which is indicated by the next longest hash mark. Each half is divided again in half, giving the inch four equal sections that are quarters. These are indicated by the next smaller hash marks. Don't be afraid to count the marks. Remember you are using the ruler for measuring and accuracy. Sometimes when I use a ruler on the computer, I still point to the marks with a pencil or my finger when counting, just to be sure.

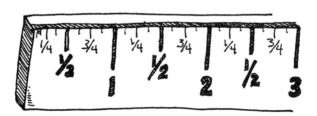

Fraction-Decimal Equivalents of an Inch

There may be times when it is necessary to convert fractions of an inch measured with a ruler into decimals for use in a computer application. One half of an inch (½) is the same as .5. One-quarter of an inch (¼) is the same as .25. One-eighth of an inch is the same as .125. But what about the rest? Use the following list of decimal equivalents to help with other conversions:

1/64	.015625	11/32	.34375	43/64	.671875
1/32	.03125	23/64	.359375	11/16	.6875
3/64	.046875	3/8	.375	45/64	.703125
1/16	.0625	25/64	.390625	23/32	.71875
5/64	.078125	13/32	.40625	47/64	.734375
3/32	.09375	27/64	.421875	3/4	.75
7/64	.109375	7/16	.4375	49/64	.765625
1/8	.125	29/64	.453125	25/32	.78125
9/64	.140625	15/32	.46875	51/64	.796875
5/32	.15625	31/64	.484375	13/16	.8125
11/64	.171875	1/2	.5	53/64	.828125
3/16	.1875	33/64	.515625	27/32	.84375
13/64	.203125	17/32	.53125	55/64	.859375
7/32	.21875	35/64	.546875	7/6	.875
15/64	.234375	9/16	.5625	57/64	.890625
1/4	.25	37/64	.578125	29/32	.90625
17/64	.265625	19/32	.59375	59/64	.921875
9/32	.28125	39/64	.609375	15/16	.9375
19/64	.296875	5/8	.625	61/64	.953125
5/16	.3125	41/64	.640625	31/32	.96875
21/64	.328125	21/32	.65625	63/64	.984375

Basic One-, Two-, and Three-Point Perspective

Even if you major in an area in which you will never draw, in which you work with computers or cameras, there may be a day when you have to get an idea across to a client or a fellow worker quickly. You don't have to draw complicated city scenes or futuristic space colonies, but your understanding of basic perspective may help you get your point across effectively. The ability to draw a simple box in perspective is a good skill to have. The ability to draw complex Escher-like environments is a great skill to have, even if it is only for art that you create for your own enjoyment.

When drawing in perspective, you are always taking the vantage point of a particular viewer. Establishing eye level or a horizon line is determined by the height of the viewer. So if you're drawing from the vantage point of a child, your eye level will be closer to the ground than it would be from the eye level of a professional basketball player.

One-Point Perspective

In one-point perspective, a single vanishing point is placed on the horizon or eye level line. The vanishing point is the place on the horizon where an object moving away from you will disappear from your vision. Think of the classic one-point perspective view looking down the train tracks. The tracks disappear at the vanishing point on the horizon. The tracks fade to one point in the distance.

250

251

You can add objects to the picture and use the same vanishing point to help maintain a consistent view. Keep the objects that the viewer can see the top of below the eye-level line. Things that are taller than the viewer are placed or extend above the eye-level line.

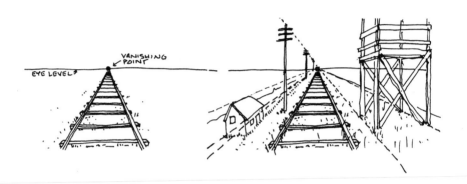

Two-Point Perspective

In two-point perspective there are two vanishing points placed on the horizon or eye-level line. The vanishing points should be placed far apart on the paper. When you can see two sides of an object, looking down one side as far as you can until you reach the horizon is where you will place one point. Do the same looking down the other side. Place a vertical line perpendicular to the horizon line representing the corner of the object closest to you.

Think of a view looking down at a warehouse from a roof-top across the street.

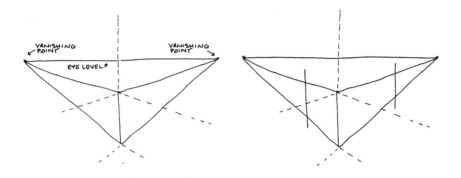

The vertical line is placed below the horizon line, because the view is one of looking down, or below eye level. Additional perpendicular vertical lines to the left or right of the closest corner allow you to define an end to how far the object will extend.

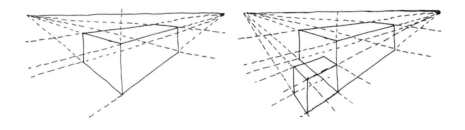

In two-point perspective the horizon line and verticals are always perpendicular to each other. All other lines extend to one of the vanishing points.

Three-Point Perspective

In three-point perspective there are three vanishing points, two are placed on the horizon or eye-level line and one is placed on a vertical line perpendicular to the horizon. The vanishing points should be placed far apart on the paper. Three-point perspective is similar to two-point perspective with the addition of the height or depth of the object. These are also affected and get smaller as they get farther away.

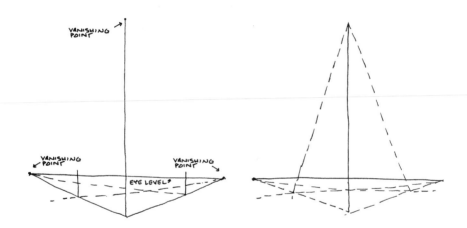

Unlike two point perspective, the only vertical line perpendicular to the horizon is the line of the closest corner to you. The other lines extend to the vanishing point on the vertical line. Use three-point perspective when you are looking up or down an object or for exaggerated views.

254

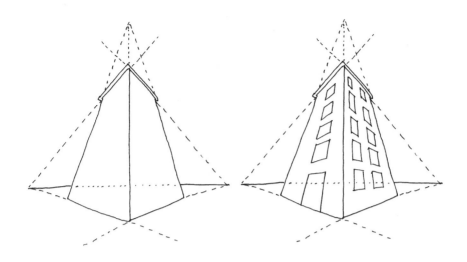

Even simple drawings of different perspective views, different eye levels, and different vanishing point placements can lead to new ways of approaching or presenting a project.

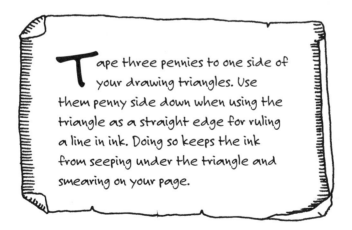

Tape three pennies to one side of your drawing triangles. Use them penny side down when using the triangle as a straight edge for ruling a line in ink. Doing so keeps the ink from seeping under the triangle and smearing on your page.

LETTERS AND TYPE

There will be times that lettering or type will be a component of your work, even if you are not a graphic designer. It is important to at least have a basic understanding of type, ways to generate it, and ways of using it to your advantage and not to your detriment.

Typography

If a course in typography is not in your curriculum, investigate some of the many good books and Web sites covering the subject. Some of the worst graphic design comes from creative people who don't understand type. Just take a look at some of the flyers hanging on almost any bulletin board. Don't be afraid to use type in your work, it can be a great decorative element or a powerful communication tool.

Some basic definitions of type anatomy follow, but realize this is just the tip of the iceberg. Some design students will have multiple courses dedicated strictly to typography. There are graphic designers who work exclusively with text and others who even specialize in type design. Will you be one of them?

256

arm—a horizontal stroke

ascender—the part of a lowercase letter that rises above its body or x height

baseline—the imaginary line that letters rest on

body height—the complete area covered by all uppercase and lowercase letters in a font

cap height—the height a capital letter from baseline

counter—the enclosed or partially enclosed part of a letter

descender—the part of a lowercase letter that dips below the baseline or x height

italic—type that is slanted

lowercase—small letters

sans serif—refers to letters without serifs

serif—the small decorative counter stroke at the end of a stem or stroke, refers to letters with serifs

stem—the most distinctive vertical stroke of a letter

uppercase—capital letters

x height—the height of lowercase letters without ascenders or descenders, the measure of the letter x

Hand Lettering

Digital design technology has taken its toll on the art forms of calligraphy and hand lettering. There was a time not so long ago when type or lettering was either set with metal type or hand drawn. Letters on posters, show cards, billboards, signs, even the sides of trucks were hand drawn or painted. Speedball pens, steel brushes, lettering brushes, and chisel tip magic markers were the tools used.

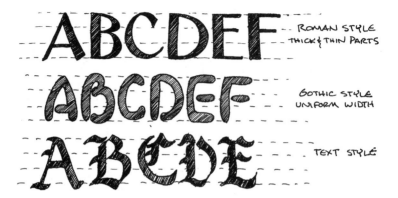

Today, a computer, a piece of software, and an output device have taken the lion's share of this work. As a result, the use of lettering tools has become a specialty area. Some universities and wedding houses still keep good calligraphers busy. Invitations to formal affairs and many university diplomas are still hand lettered using a speedball or lettering pen and a bottle of ink.

Illustrated type or text is another art form that is seen less since the advent of desktop publishing. There was a time when mimeographed hand-drawn flyers were commonplace. The screen printing of hand-drawn art was an option for short runs of posters. The combination of illustrated lettering and digital printing is another way to give a personal touch to an ordinary flyer. Bradley Keough's flyer for a small music festival is one such example.

Making An Image/Reference File

No matter what area of art you decide to concentrate on, there will be times that you will find yourself in need of reference material for a project. Maybe it is a term paper or research paper. Perhaps it is sound or music for a performance or presentation. Sometimes it will be visual reference for inspiration and accuracy. Some material will be fairly accessible, some will require a more concerted effort to find. One way to be ready for future needs is to prepare now.

The image reference file is not a new idea. Many art libraries have a room or collection of picture reference material. It may be old magazine covers, photographs, even newspaper clippings. Major libraries have such picture collections. These collections can run deep with obscure items. A freelance project for the National Lifesaving Championships started a search at the Philadelphia Free Library's Print and Picture Collection. A folder two inches thick emerged from behind the counter, a folder that could be taken out like a book with a library card. But what if you are not near a great library? There is always the Internet. But having your own collection allows you to work with items that appeal to your sense of aesthetics. The sooner

260

you start, the sooner you will have a reference collection of your own to draw from.

But how do you start? Where do you look? What do you save? There is no telling what your needs might be. A 1967 Mustang, a smoking pipe like Sherlock Holmes used, a palm tree, a raccoon, even a Revolutionary War uniform. Indeed, where to begin? Try using an outline approach. Start with major topics and subjects then start breaking them down into subcategories. Folders work fine. Sub-category folders can reside inside their respective major topic folder. This file will grow into a valuable resource.

And what do you fill it with? Where do you find all these great pictures? Magazines are a great place to start. Watch the paper recycling. If you see a house for sale, people will be moving soon and they may not want to move everything. Family members are good. Put the word out that you want magazines about food, sports, fashion, hobbies. They are all good. Flip through them, look at the ads and the articles. Tear carefully, cut, trim, and then file.

Setting Up Your Image Files

Begin your own photo collection. Take pictures when on vacation or traveling. If you are at a parade, a concert, a fair, a car show, take pictures. If there is a pow-wow, a reenactment, or an anniversary of some historic event, check it out and take your camera.

Your major topics may change according to your needs, major, or interests. In fact it may look nothing like this, but here is an outline to use as reference and help get your image file started and organized:

I. Housing
    A. Exterior
    B. Interior
    C. Furnishings

II. Nature
    A. Gardens and Flowers
    B. Trees
    C. Snow and Water
    D. Miscellaneous

III. Animals
    A. Domestic
    B. Wild
    C. Horses
    D. Miscellaneous

IV. Sports
    A. Events
    B. Individual
    C. Team

V. Transportation
    A. Aircraft
    B. Automobiles
    C. Boats
    D. Public
    E. Miscellaneous

VI. People
    A. Children
    B. Men
    C. Women
    D. Groups
    E. Miscellaneous

VII. Costume
    A. Women's Fashions

    B. Uniforms
    C. Period
    D. Miscellaneous
VIII. Entertainment
    A. Music
    B. Dance
    C. Theater
    D. Miscellaneous

IX. Art and Science
    A. Art
    B. Science
    C. Miscellaneous

 X. Industry
    A. Stores and Offices
    B. Farming
    C. Industry

XI. Foreign
    A. Europe
    B. Asia
    C. Africa
    D. South America
    E. Islands
    F. Miscellaneous

XII. Miscellaneous
    A. Church and School
    B. Disaster
    C. Government
    D. Regional America
    E. Street Scenes

Review your files periodically. Know what is in them.
Encourage your friends to make files as well. Share the
files, trade pictures, old magazines, photos. Two or three
serious art student image files will yield vast quantities
of helpful reference material.

FINDING RESEARCH MATERIALS AND INSPIRATION

There will be times in your life when you will need to do research. Not just open a book research or an Internet search, but serious research. When this happens, do not limit yourself to your local library or favorite search engine. Communication technology has advanced to the point that sources of information and inspiration that once were out of reach are now available literally at your fingertips. But it has also made it easy to bypass the extra effort to go and see things up close and personal. I've seen Van Gogh's painting "Starry Night" reproduced hundreds of times, but when I saw the real deal it was a whole different experience. No blue reproduced in print can match Van Gogh's blue on the original. Make the extra effort if you can.

Libraries

Your school library offers more than what you see on the shelves. There may be a rare collection that is not on display or needs special permission to access. Other schools and universities also have their own special collections and resources. Generally with your student ID card you can visit and research at other school libraries, but you may not be able to borrow from them. Each library has something different to offer. The research section at each one will be geared a little differently.

Through interlibrary loan programs a student can take advantage of the books and special collections at other

264

schools. Allow extra time for this process, as the item you require may already be checked out. Then there is the time it takes to process and deliver the item. Check with your school librarian. It may be necessary to do some paperwork and talk to some administrators, but the effort is well worth it.

Do not limit yourself to school libraries. Public libraries, even in small towns can hold wonderful collections. Rich people, famous people, rich and famous people leave collections to libraries and museums. Some of these collections are well publicized; some of them are forgotten treasures. Some may be discovered through hard work and research; some may be stumbled on accidentally. Share this information with your faculty and classmates. It may prove advantageous to take a study partner with you when you research, as there may be an abundance of information at your disposal.

Museums

Museums are not just for or about art, although many of the world's greatest museums are art museums. As an art student these will probably be the museums you will be utilizing and visiting. But don't forget about the other museums. Natural history museums, maritime museums, living farm museums, transportation museums, and medical museums. There are museums for just about every area of interest. They may not be big, or well funded, or even convenient, but you would be surprised at the museums out there. These places all can give you access to that something extra that can open new doors in your work.

Some museums also have libraries and special collections. While that might not be what they are known for, the information desk can help you find those extras that can take a project from good to great. Read the brochures that are found at the museum information desk. Ask questions of the people who work there.

Use your student ID for discounts at museums and supply stores. Don't be afraid to ask any place you are spending money if they give student discounts. Ten percent here, ten percent there adds up.

WHEN TRAVELING

Slide lectures and pictures in art history books are ways to see important works of art located in different states or countries. But there may be noticeable differences in the quality of color represented in the reproductions that you view. These differences can vary so much that you may be confused as to what the real color of a painting actually is. One way to clear that confusion is to go and see the real work. This may be as a pilgrimage or quest; it may be as a side trip while on vacation. Seeing your favorite work of art in person for the first time is one of the great eye-opening experiences any artist can have. Of course, museum trips should not be limited to just major museums and your favorite artists. Some smaller museums also hold real gems and masterpieces in their collections.

266

An Unexpected Pleasure

Whether traveling for work or pleasure, I try to make it a practice to visit some of that area's art museums or galleries. Recently while in San Diego for a conference, I visited the art museum located there, which is situated in a beautiful park setting. The headlining exhibition was Degas Bronzes, about 70 bronze studies of dancers and horses. This exhibition in itself was a great treat, but the Philadelphia Museum of Art (my local museum) just had a huge Degas show, and while the San Diego exhibition was a nice complement to that, I was still experiencing some Degas saturation. What I also found there was a smaller exhibit of drawings and woodcut prints by the Japanese artist Hokusai. Those works, specifically the ink drawings, blew me away. My first visit to San Diego was for a conference. While there I met many professionals in my field and visited a great Degas show, but I will probably remember the trip most for the Hokusai drawings I saw.

WAYS TO VIEW AN EXHIBIT AT A MUSEUM OR GALLERY

✔ <u>Do not touch</u>, unless invited to by the artist or exhibition space.

✔ Be mindful of others viewing the exhibit. Do not hog the view, but be sure to get a good look at the work. Look at the works from up close, back a few steps, and then from farther away yet again, if applicable.

✔ Turn off your cell phone.

✔ Talk quietly.

✔ Do not eat or drink unless invited to.

✔ When entering a salon or room in a gallery, go right to the work in the room that commands your interest first. Go through the entire exhibit this way, then view the exhibit again from the beginning to the end, reading all text displays and sidebars related to the exhibit. Read them in the sequence they were intended to be read.

✔ Try renting an audio tour next time you go to an exhibit at a museum. Try taking one of the museum's guided tours with a museum docent.

When was the last time you visited a museum? Where was it? If you are a serious art student, probably you will have already visited the closest art museum to you, maybe as field trips with school, maybe as family outings. You may be well versed in the collections found there and even have your own personal favorite works and artists. But not all students have the opportunities to get to museums. The closest museum may be hundreds of miles away, making a field trip unrealistic. Perhaps you are the only family member interested in the arts, in which case a family trip may not be in the cards. It is imperative that those students who have never been get to an art museum ASAP. Take advantage of tours or go with classmates. Wander around with eyes wide open; absorb as much as possible.

Whether you like the work on display is not the issue. Not everyone will. But seeing the work at least gives the opportunity to know whether one likes it. Any work can inspire. Some may give way to a new approach or way of thinking. Others may give examples of ways not to go. The important thing is to get out and see the work that is hanging on the walls, in the showcases, and on the pedestals of the museums and galleries of the world. For those students who are not world travelers, look locally. Smaller cities and towns, even rural areas have museums and other places of inspiration and interest. Again, it may take a little work to find them, but they are there.

MUSEUMS GALORE

Again using Philadelphia and the Delaware Valley as an example, not only is the world-class Philadelphia Museum of Art located here, but the Barnes Collection and the Rodin Museum are here also. Then there is the nearby Brandywine River Museum, which contains a great collection of works by Andrew Wyeth, his father N. C. Wyeth, and his son, Jamie Wyeth. The Delaware Art Museum in Wilmington has wonderful collections of pre-Raphaelite paintings as well as Howard Pyle illustrations. There is even a library there for research. There are the Woodmere, Mutter, and Michner museums, the Pennsylvania Academy of Fine Arts, the University of Pennsylvania Archeological Museum, the sculpture gardens of the Morris Arboretum, and the Old City gallery district. These are just off the top of my head. The list would grow by simply opening a phonebook.

REAL WORLD AND VIRTUAL PLACES

Some of these places are obvious and impossible to miss. The Louvre in Paris, the Metropolitan Museum of Art in New York City, the Hermitage in St. Petersburg, Russia. Some are tucked away in corners and require a little more work to find. When traveling, especially overseas, try a travel guide for your destination. These can be found in the travel section of a bookstore. If you are looking more locally, try the phonebook. Look in the yellow pages under "Museums." Seems obvious, but you would be surprised how many people would not think of it. Try the local chamber of commerce, office of travel and tourism, or visitor center. Try the public library or your own school library. The reference or research librarian will be happy to help you.

Then there is the Internet and the search engines found there. It is easy to use a favorite search engine, but try different ones from time to time. Also when conducting an Internet search, try doing advanced searches keying in additional words. Try phrasing your choice of words differently. Save the results of your searches, or at least bookmark the pages for future reference. It is also important to remember that all information found on the Internet or World Wide Web is not necessarily fact. Anyone can publish and promote a Web site and make it look real official. If you are planning on making a special trip to a place that you found on the Internet, call first and make sure that it exists, it is what you think it is, and has the hours of access you require. When possible, go to official Web sites. Not everything is a dot-com. Some that are government run will be ".gov" sites, some that are nonprofit are ".org" sites. Do your homework. Make your trip worth the effort.

271

Ask teachers, professors, relatives, and friends about their experiences and the places they have visited. Maybe they have favorites that they can share. Maybe they are looking to take a trip to a new museum or gallery. Not every place of inspiration has to be a museum. Remember the scene in "Rocky" (the original "Rocky") in which he wakes up and chugs those raw eggs. Then the "Italian Stallion" goes for a run through the Italian Market of south Philadelphia. The sights, sounds, and smells found there can be inspirational. The lighthouse at Cape Hatteras, North Carolina, the Chinatown section of San Francisco, the Boboli gardens of Florence, Italy, a scenic train ride through the Alps, a walk in the park. Inspiration can be anywhere you want it to be. If you make the effort to look for it, chances are you will find it.

For those who have a problem with traveling, many museums have high quality books published containing its collections as well as the catalogs of the special exhibitions that it has offered. There are books dedicated to different regions and the areas of interest that they offer. If you cannot afford them, ask your school librarian if the school can purchase them for the library. If budget allows, and many times it will, your interests and input may contribute to the holdings of your school's library.

NOTES:

Campbell's Soup Can, Andy Warhol, 1964

Glossary

advisors Those who give advice. Can refer to people whose job it is to advise you or people whose judgment you trust and look to when you are in doubt as to what to do. Most colleges have advisors available to students and many even assign faculty members to be advisors to the students in the department.

calligraphic Term used in reference to calligraphy or the art of hand lettering.

camaraderie Deep friendship, brotherhood, being together with friends and peers. The feeling of belonging to a group.

carpal tunnel syndrome A condition often associated with working on a computer, usually affecting the hand that works the mouse. The nerves between the hand and wrist become inflamed, causing numbness in the fingertips and eventually pain and loss of movement. Can be remedied with vitamins, a brace, and rest.

chain of command   The order of importance by rank. For example, in school, a teacher supervises a student, a principal or department chair supervises a teacher. In the military a private reports to a sergeant, a sergeant reports to a lieutenant, and so on.

chiropractor   A doctor who specializes in the alignment of the bones of the spine and other parts of the body and how that alignment can affect one's overall health.

chronological   The order in which something happened.

comp   A developed sketch of an idea for a visual project. Comps come in a variety of stages of completeness. Usually following the initial thumbnail sketch, the comp answers layout and color questions before a final is attempted. Tighter comps are presented to clients during the design process for approval of an idea and direction.

conceptual   Dealing with a concept or an idea. Usually refers to artwork that relies on the idea to carry the message more than the image itself.

conté   A drawing crayon usually available in black, sepia, and white; similar to chalk or charcoal.

copyright   The legal right and process of protecting original creative work, whether it is art, music, or the written word. Work protected by copyright is marked with © symbol, the year, and artist's name, for example ©2004 Jeffrey Otto.

curriculum   Educational course work geared toward a particular field of study.

Day-Timer A brand name of personal calendar and appointment book often used to identify all personal or business appointment books. These books usually contain areas for phone numbers, addresses, a calculator, and a calendar.

deadline Time and day that a project is due for completion and or delivery. Get used to it.

digital media Devices used for the storage of projects created using computers or computer-based technology.

digitize To transfer something from the analog world to the computer or digital world. To transform to digital form.

discordant Unmatching, disagreeing, using elements that clash with each other.

embellish To add to, to further describe something, to decorate.

enlightenment A state of heightened awareness. Usually refers to a spiritual state of mind. Can also be used in reference to knowledge.

ergonomics The science that deals with the design and arrangement of tools to minimize fatigue and maximize efficiency and safety for the people who use them.

extracurricular activities School-sponsored or school-supported activities that are not part of the regular curriculum.

field The professional world as related to the major of study.

flatfiles Studio furniture designed with shallow drawers usually between 2 and 4 inches deep for storage of paper and flat artwork.

freelancer One who freelances. An independent worker who hires out services to those who need them. Most illustration work is freelance. Art directors hire illustrators when they need them.

general education The coursework in a curriculum that deals with the liberal arts and not the major course of study. Different curricula require different percentages of general education courses, examples of which include World Literature, Philosophy, and Western Civilization.

grad school Graduate school; usually refers to degree programs beyond the bachelor degree, such as Master of Arts, Master of Science, or Master of Fine Arts.

hierarchy A point of order that follows a sequence from lowest to highest. A grouping of people according to rank. See chain of command.

hybrids Custom-made from a combination of more than one existing element.

ignorant Missing or void of the information needed to understand something.

illuminate To add visuals to text to help clarify the message. Can also be the addition of an illustration to further explain or capture attention. The illuminated manuscripts of the Middle Ages are a good example of artwork working to aid in the message of text. To make clear or to decorate.

industrial designer   An artist who designs objects used by people in their everyday lives or in their workplace. From telephones to toasters, lighting fixtures to litter boxes, all are designed by the industrial designer.

intuitive   Doing something without even thinking about it. Knowing something so thoroughly that it is second nature. Intuition.

licensing   The rights to an image or object that can be sold for the purpose of reproduction, use, and possible sales. The permission to use the licensed item.

linear   In a straightforward method of presentation. A logical progression of presentation. Relating to sequential development.

loner   Someone who spends most of the time in his or her own company and is not really a part of any group of close friends.

Luddite   A group of 19th-century workers who destroyed machinery as a protest. Someone who opposes technology or technological advancement.

mock-up   Much like a comp. An abbreviated version of a more definite idea. Usually a rough presentation to get the basic idea across. A model built for study or display.

multimedia   The use of multiple media; the mixing of audio and visual elements in the same project. Other art forms may include animation, video, and interactive computer programming.

networking   Meeting people and organizations to further career paths. Establishing a network of professionals who can establish a quid pro quo (I'll scratch your back, you scratch my back) relationship to the mutual benefit of both.

nonlinear Unlike linear, nonlinear deals with multiple parts of a larger project that can be mixed and matched in different order, not necessarily following a specific order or sequence.

peers Friends and people from the same classification as you. In school, your peers are fellow students, not the faculty. In sports, your peers are your teammates, not your coach. People with whom you associate who are at the same tier as you.

PhotoShop Popular digital imaging software package used for scanning, coloring, photo retouching, painting, and image manipulation. A staple for any artist who works in the digital arena.

plagiarism Stealing of an idea or work. Claiming ownership or authorship to a particular work especially but not limited to written works. At the college or university level, being accused and convicted of plagiarism usually results in expulsion from school.

priorities The order of importance given to a number of issues or projects. Priorities can change from day to day. The top or first priority is usually the most important thing that you must take care of on a given day.

procrastinate To put off doing something until later.

registration week The week during session (semester, trimester, or quarter) when classes for the next session are picked and signed up for.

Renaissance The rebirth. The period of history in Europe that identifies the time after the Middle Ages and the reawakening of the arts and culture.

rubbings   The images transferred from a relief or raised surface onto a paper or cloth by rubbing a crayon or charcoal on the paper as it is held against the raised surface.

scratchboard   A process for making line art. Using tools that make different size and shape lines, lines are made by scraping away the black surface of the board revealing white. Can give an engraved look or feel to the drawing.

sequential   A logical order that shows a series of related items in the order in which they occur. One after another.

specs   Short for "specifications." In art, usually refers to the size, orientation, and any other specific conditions pertaining to the piece of art involved.

Spell-check   Name of software tool that checks spelling in a word-processing document. Also used in reference to spell-checking feature in other software applications.

study groups   Informal or assigned groupings of students that meet to discuss content of class for study purposes. A good way to see how others observe or process the same information.

subliminal   Suggestion delivered to viewer in such a small dose as to not be recognized, yet that can plant a seed of an idea into the subconscious.

success   To attain one's goals. Goals can change during different times of your life, so definitions of success will probably change also.

survive To last and continue on when others have not been able to. To continue moving forward during and after a difficult situation.

symbolism In art, the use of certain colors or objects in a work that represent something else. A dog might represent loyalty; a lion might represent royalty.

tortillons A type of rolled paper stub used for blending and smearing pencil, conté, or charcoal.

vellum A type of drawing paper used for drafting. Can be translucent. Also refers to a finish on paper, not smooth. Also writing or drawing surface made from lambskin.

Wiener Werkstatte Refers to a period or movement in art associated with the artists from the Vienna area during the turn of the 20th century.

work for hire Contracted work whereby an artist is hired for his or her skill to perform a specific function. The artist receives no credit or rights to the work produced.

work on spec Work done on speculation or on the chance that there may be payment or a reward later. "Do this for me now and if it hits big, you'll be the main artist and get all the work later." (Never really a good idea.)

Index

INDEX

INDEX